Contents

2   *Foreword*
     Ian G Robertson, Director, National Army [

5   *Task Force Falklands*
     Field Marshal The Lord Bramall

19   *The Land Battle*
     Major–General Julian Thompson

40   *The Army's Infantry and Armoured Reconnaissance Forces*
     Brigadier Hew Pike

49   *The Gunners*
     Major–General Brian Pennicott

55   *Advance Force Operations: The SAS*
     Major–General Michael Rose

61   *Unsung Heroes*
     Marion Harding

76   *The Royal Army Ordnance Corps*
     Brigadier Anthony Welch

81   *The Legacy*
     Major–General Sir David Thorne

89   *Ten Years On - The Literature of the Falklands War*
     Dr Linda Washington

103 *Chronology*

105 *Order of Battle*

107 *Helicopter availability during the Land Battle*

108 *Glossary*

110 *Index*

Foreword

Ian G Robertson, Director, National Army Museum

The Tenth Anniversary in 1992 of the Campaign by which British Forces drove Argentine troops from the Falkland Islands presented particular opportunities to the staff of the National Army Museum. First, the Special Exhibition mounted during the summer months of 1992 marked this significant Anniversary by putting on display items from the Museum's own permanent collections as well as material kindly lent by others. It is hoped that this will enable our holdings to be augmented further by the donation of items, the authenticity of which is not in doubt. Secondly, the production of this Publication allowed an interesting addition to be made to the growing volume of Campaign Literature, by putting into print the recollections, (which it is thought will be of considerable interest to historians in the future), of invited participants. As with all campaigns, nonsense tends to be written to some degree and it is appropriate that the National Army Museum should provide the opportunity to those who had taken part to set out their views in their own style for the benefit of all.

Rather than opt for a chronological re-examination of the crisis through April, May and June 1982, it was decided to look at the series of problems it posed for the British Army, with the much-appreciated help of some of the leading participants in the repossession and restoration of the Islands, who have applied ten years of historical reflection to their own experiences. From his key perspective as the then Chief of the General Staff, Field Marshal The Lord Bramall considers the British response to the Argentine invasion; Major-General Julian Thompson analyses the land battle in which he commanded 3 Commando Brigade; Brigadier Hew Pike, then Commanding Officer of the 3rd Battalion The Parachute Regiment, examines the role of the Army's infantry and armoured reconnaissance forces; the particular problems facing the Royal Artillery are recalled by Major-General Brian Pennicott, who was to witness General Menendez's final surrender; the contribution made by the Special Air Service in Advance Force Operations is revealed by Major-General Michael Rose, this being the first occasion upon which the representative of the SAS Regiment has put pen to paper concerning its activities during the War; Brigadier Anthony Welch recalls the huge logistic operation behind the fighting, while Major-General Sir David Thorne describes how the long process of restoring the Islands got under way. A special debt of gratitude is due to all the above authors who gave up their time to accept the invitation to contribute to this Publication. There are in addition two contributions from members of the staff of the National Army Museum: Marion Harding, of the Department of Archives, Photographs, Film and Sound, considers the essential role played by the Army Corps, drawing on an under-utilized source, namely, Regimental and Corps Publications, while this Volume's Editor, Dr Linda Washington, discusses the emerging trends in the literature surrounding the Campaign.

Guided by David Smurthwaite, Assistant Director (Museum Services), the Special Exhibition was organized by a project team under the leadership of Dr Linda Washington, assisted by Mrs Marion Harding, Martin Hinchcliffe and Alastair Massie. Many members of the Collections Division also contributed their valued specialist expertise to the success of the Exhibition: Sylvia Hopkins, Lesley Smurthwaite, Natalia Wieczorek, Ian Maine, Carolyn Charles, Michael Baldwin, Keith Miller, Emma Bond, Peter Boyden, Clare Wright, Angela Kelsall, Jenny Spencer-Smith and Michael Ball.

The National Army Museum's Museum Services Division bore a particularly heavy burden during the preparation of the Exhibition, coinciding as it did with a major refurbishment project in the Permanent Galleries. The Falklands display was designed by Amy Bridgman, with the assistance of Sarah Godwin, and the publication by Paul Greenland. Paul Tew, Ray Seabrook and Ian Lee undertook the considerable construction work involved. The photographs accompanying the display and contained in this publication were taken by Ian Jones, Nigel Armstrong and Carl Critchley. Conservation of exhibits was carried out by Adrian Carlton, Martin Hinchcliffe, Vincent Prior and Erika Arnold. All sectors of the Museum eventually became involved in this absorbing task. The Museum Secretary, David Langham, who served with the RAOC in the Falklands, loaned material from his own collection, while Mr John Mills of the Warding Staff helped to acquire some of the items used to illustrate this volume. The text of the Publication and the Special Exhibition captions were typed by Kate Plowman.

To mount a display covering such a recent episode of Britain's military history one is very much dependent on the help and co-operation of the Ministry of Defence, as well as the units and individuals who served in the Falklands during the Campaign and afterwards. Particular thanks are due to the staff of the Logistic Executive at Andover, including Mr D Ashdown, Major P Burke, Mr J Finch, Mr C Goodeson, Lieutenant-Colonel A A King, Major E D Marlow, Squadron Leader D R McIntyre, and Major D Moore. The staff of the Royal Military Academy at Sandhurst, including Lieutenant-Colonel N E Menzies and WO2 G Colville, provided assistance to the Museum's Department of Uniforms, Badges and Medals. I am also grateful for the help of several national and regimental museums, including Mr P Attwood of the Coins and Medals Department of the British Museum; Ms Jane Carmichael, Mr R H Hamilton, Mr M D Moody, Ms Angela Weight and Ms Jenny Wood of the Imperial War Museum; Mrs Diana Andrews of the Airborne Forces Museum; Lieutenant-Colonel D A Armitage and Major L Smith of the Museum of Army Flying; Major A W Kersting of the Household Cavalry Museum; Mrs Carol Mason of the Gurkha Museum; Brigadier K A Timbers and Mr S C Walter of the Royal Artillery Institution; Lieutenant-Colonel M H G Young and Mr F O'Connell of the Royal Corps of Transport Museum; the Historical Branch (Army); and Dr M Nicholls of Cambridge University Library.

Many other individuals and representatives of units who took part in the conflict or helped to rebuild the Islands also spared the time to co-operate with the Museum: Major P Bates; Major D G Benest; Brigadier D Brownson; Major J Child; Mr D Copeland; Major S M Drennan; Major M A Easey; Lieutenant-Colonel R Elliott; Colour-Sergeant Frost; Captain J A Field; Staff-Sergeant M J Haines; Colonel P C R Howes; Lieutenant-Colonel C M StG Kirke; Miss Linda Kitson; Lieutenant G Matthews; Major P M McComas; Sergeant S C Newland; Major G Pugh; Major P Simmonds; Colonel E Southby-Tailyour; Captain A D Stevens; Major A Tahapa; Major-General N F Vaux; Captain N C B Wilkes; Lieutenant-Colonel D R D'A Willis; Major I Winfield; Major R E Whyte. Thanks are also due to Mr Ian Brownlee of GEC Ferranti which developed some of the new technology used in the War, and to the staff of Vanguard Engineering whose skilful transport of large vehicles and weapons make such Special Exhibitions possible. The Press was also helpful in tracking down obscure photographs and I would like to acknowledge the strenuous efforts made by Denis Hart of Express Newspapers and Bill Stroud of *Soldier* magazine.

In conclusion, it is appropriate, having thanked everyone for their assistance, to remember that, in discharging the National Army Museum's remit under its Royal Charter to concern itself with the history and traditions of the British Army, the latter has frequently involved personal sacrifice. Therefore, if the Special Exhibition and this Publication have any merit then they are dedicated to the memory of those who did not return home in 1982.

April 1992

4

Great Britain, the Falkland Islands and South Georgia

Task Force Falklands

Field Marshal The Lord Bramall (Chief of the General Staff July 1979–October 1982)

When the Falklands were unexpectedly invaded and taken over by the Argentines on 2 April 1982, I suppose the immediate feeling in this country was one of anger, frustration and shame, with perhaps a sneaking suspicion that, important as were the principles of self–determination for the Falkland Islands and aggression not paying, there was precious little, militarily, we could actually do about it, even if the political will was there, which in the past it might not have been. The Islands were, after all, so far away, so comparatively close to the Argentine air bases and the weather was getting progressively more atrocious.

But that the Government had to do something there was little doubt. A dramatic and acrimonious debate in the House of Commons on 3 April had made it perfectly clear that the Government was not only being held to blame for failing to deter the Argentines and allowing the Islands to be invaded in the first place, but that if it was to retain the confidence of the House, it would be expected to make amends by getting the Argentines out as quickly as possible. Both therefore politics and the public, and the honour, credibility and even, perhaps, future of the country were demanding action to achieve repossession of the Falkland Islands; and it would clearly be up to the Chiefs of Staff, under the Chief of the Defence Staff, to produce coherent advice and, if possible, a practical plan to bring this about.

Moreover, as we, the Chiefs of Staff, started to dig into our resources and put together the Task Force with the unstinting commitment of all three Services, it dawned on us that we were giving the Government a pretty decent poker hand with which to back diplomacy and economic measures – a hand quite good enough to enter the game and raise the ante and make it more expensive for the Argentines to stay in the game. Of course, it was not the perfect hand because of the distance away at which we were going to have to fight and the fact that we would have to do so under the noses of the powerful Argentine Air Force, whose bases could not really be kept out of action, whatever we did.

But the important thing was to get a task force sailing urgently for the South Atlantic, for neither military action nor repossession through negotiation would be possible without our manifest ability to project our power and will into the area in question, and over this much of the credit is due to the First Sea Lord, Admiral Sir Henry Leach. As early as the evening of 1 April, and on his own initiative, the Admiral had gone to the Prime Minister and told her he could sail, virtually immediately, a formidable task force which could be deployed in the area of the Falklands in some three weeks' time and that, if hostilities occurred, the Fleet could look after itself in the face of any Argentine naval and air attacks. This was a courageous act and was exactly what the Prime Minister wanted to hear.

So it was that in an astonishingly short time – indeed in well under a week, on the following Monday, 5 April – a task force of over 100 ships, and building up to 28,000 men, began to steam south under the British flag, joining up with a smaller group already dispatched from Gibraltar on 2 April. It was by any standards a formidable feat which was only made possible by the First Sea Lord making it clear to his staff and subordinates that all obstacles were to be overcome, by the immense support given to the Royal Navy by the other two Services, and by the fantastic co–operation given by shipbuilders (to convert merchant ships) and by dockers in a revival of the Battle of Britain spirit; and also by the fortunate ability to use the staging facilities of the United States–run, but British–owned, Ascension Island, near the Equator, as a forward operating base and for the topping up of all those items which might have been forgotten in the rush to get away!

With the Task Force sailing south to emphasize Britain's determination not to accept Argentine occupation of the Falklands, and while intense diplomatic activity started through the United Nations and under the tireless and energetic auspices of the US Secretary of State, General Alexander Haig, the Chiefs of Staff were able to apply themselves to the various military options available, the pre-

cise balance of force which might be needed, and generally to the degrees of risk and opportunity which would develop as events unfolded. To do this we met daily, or sometimes even twice daily, under Admiral of the Fleet Sir Terence Lewin (now Lord Lewin), the Chief of the Defence Staff.

At these meetings the discussions and arguments ranged forcefully and comprehensively through the whole gamut of the crisis. Once decisions had been taken on the initial composition of the Task Force, which had to include sufficient ground troops to effect, if necessary, an initial landing on the Falklands, the first major issue to be addressed urgently was the question of the chain of command. After that, the Chiefs had to establish, with the Defence Committee (Falklands) – in effect a War Cabinet – to what extent we were now to be actually at war with the Argentines and, in consequence, what restraints would have to be imposed on our forces by means of clearly defined Rules of Engagement; and even within such rules, how we could establish early psy-

Typical Falklands terrain: the view north–north–west from the top of Mount Harriet. *Courtesy of Lieutenant–Colonel C M StG Kirke*

chological superiority over the Argentines and seize the initiative which would be so vital for success.

Then the problem of South Georgia had to be tackled. Would it, in the face of some possible Argentine reinforcement of the island by submarine, be better to deal with this dependency first, even at the expense of delaying the arrival of the main Task Force off the Falklands? If so, what force would be needed to be preloaded and, at an early stage (probably around Ascension Island) divorced from the main Task Force, in order to make sure the job was done properly?

Finally, it would be no good sailing the Task Force until there was some clear concept as to what it might have to do when it arrived off its destination. This involved making an initial appreciation on what other land forces might be required to effect partial or total repossession of the Islands if, by then, the Argentines had not been persuaded, by our show of force or by diplomatic and economic means, to evacuate, and were prepared to put up a spirited and determined defence of the Islands, backed up by their navy and land-based aircraft. Would it be possible, under these circumstances, actually to achieve the conditions under which a landing and repossession became militarily feasible and, if not, what alternatives, such as a blockade, were open to us?

In the event, the overall command arrangements turned out, albeit a little fortuitously, to be something of a model, and in marked contrast to some disastrous combined operations of the past, such as Gallipoli in 1915 and the Norwegian campaign in 1940, in both of which faulty command arrangements had significantly contributed to failure. The approach to the Falklands was exclusively by sea, and our power could only be, therefore, projected by surface and sub-surface ships and by aircraft, which had to be, largely because of the distances away from any land bases, on ships actually accompanying the Task Force. The detailed planning

and command of the operation therefore fell properly to the Commander-in-Chief (C-in-C) Fleet, Admiral Sir John Fieldhouse (the late Lord Fieldhouse) and his joint maritime headquarters at Northwood, on the outskirts of London, where he already had integrated RAF advice in the form of Air Officer Commanding 18 Group (the Maritime Group) and could easily be provided with the necessary Land Force advice as well.

The remains of the Royal Marine barracks at Moody Brook, attacked by Argentine Special Forces in the early morning of 2 April. *Courtesy of D Langham*

Fieldhouse would then exercise his command, other than over his submarines, which would remain commanded from Northwood, through a Task Force Commander at sea, Rear Admiral 'Sandy' Woodward, who was already afloat with the group at Gibraltar as one of the Flag Officers First Flotilla. In addition, if a landing had to be effected, and once sufficient forces were established ashore, the C-in-C would have a Land Forces Commander reporting directly to him as well. The fortuitous element came in the fact that the Chief of the Defence Staff (Lewin), the Chief of the Naval Staff (Leach), the Commander-in-Chief (Fieldhouse) and the Commander of the Task Groups at sea (Woodward), had all served together recently and knew each other well.

If there were any criticisms to be levelled in hindsight at the command arrangements, they would have been in the field of the command of the Land Forces. As any repossession would involve an amphibious landing of some sort, the Royal Marines were required to be in the lead and the larger part of the initial landing force was properly to be provided by Royal Marine Commandos. The Navy, therefore, understandably insisted that the Land Forces Commander should be a senior Royal Marine officer, in this case the experienced Major–General Commando Forces, Major–General Jeremy Moore. This turned out to be an excellent choice, but the trouble was that the Navy also wanted Moore to act as the senior Land Forces planner and adviser to Fieldhouse at the Headquarters at Northwood during the initial stages of the deployment, and only to move him down to the War Zone by sea at a much later stage and with the main reserve.

The Royal Marine garrison surrenders its weapons and equipment to Argentine commandos at Port Stanley, 2 April. *Frank Spooner/Gamma*

Delegating the planning of any operations to someone who eventually has to execute those plans always has considerable merit, but, in practice and as events progressed, it became increasingly difficult to reconcile these two roles; and there turned out to be about 72 crucial hours, after the initial bridgehead had been established, when the Land Force Commander's presence was badly needed ashore at San Carlos and yet Moore was still on his way down by sea to join the Task Force. He was, therefore, out of touch with the battle and

unable to provide the immediate impetus and direction which was required. With hindsight, Moore should have handed over to the Army (or another Royal Marine) adviser somewhat earlier, or somehow travelled more quickly and thus would have been able to advise Woodward during the final deployment and approach to the landing area and, much more importantly, to command ashore at an earlier stage.

But above Task Force level there could be few criticisms. Lewin, the Chief of the Defence Staff, having first discussed the key issues with the other Chiefs of Staff and having been advised by us both on broad strategy and more detailed aspects of implementation affecting each of our three Services, would tender his own advice to the War Cabinet. There, in a perfect piece of political/military interface, he would clear the broad lines of policy and any constraints within which the military would have to operate.

He would then give the Commander–in–Chief, Fieldhouse, his general directions, aims and objectives, which left the latter free from long–range interference to plan in detail the winning of the sea and air battle, and the repossession of the Islands. It all worked extremely smoothly. Commanders in the operational area seldom found themselves suffering from an excess of back–seat driving or lacking the necessary direction as to what they could or could not do in any given set of circumstances, although the delay in the arrival in the South Atlantic of Moore did lead to some misunderstandings and delays immediately after the initial bridgehead had been secured.

The second immediate question before the Chiefs – the extent of hostilities and the Rules of Engagement which, in consequence, would be necessary for the Task Force – was an involved one. Although the Argentines had put themselves completely in the wrong by invading in the first place, and had committed a clear act of aggression, they had, as much by luck as by good and humane judgement, taken over

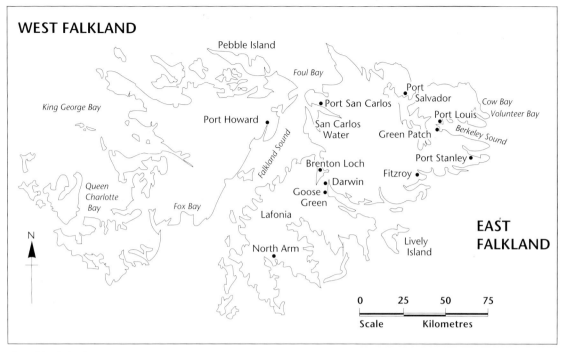

The Falkland Islands

the Falklands without causing a single British casualty. As long as there was a chance, therefore, that, under both international pressure and our own military pressure, the Argentines might be made to see the error of their ways and withdraw, the British Government was understandably reluctant to declare the start of hostilities, thus implying that our own use of force was now inevitable; or indeed to use, in any situation, any more force than (under Article 51 of the UN Charter) was absolutely necessary in achieving that withdrawal. Taking action in self–defence was, of course, and under the circumstances, perfectly legal in International Law under that UN Article. But what exactly, in this context, constituted self–defence was a debatable point when, with naval aviation and stand–off missiles, an enemy could strike a crippling blow from some distance away.

Although trying to reconcile these sometimes conflicting requirements produced a certain amount of argument in the Chiefs of Staff Committee, an agreed formula soon found favour. This established a Maritime Exclusion Zone with a radius of some two hundred miles from a central point in the Falkland Islands. Inside this, the Argentines were warned that any of their warships and auxiliaries would be assumed to be hostile and could properly be attacked. This Zone was enforced initially by the Royal Navy's nuclear submarines, the first units which could actually be got to the operational area and the presence of which, in any case, no one in Argentina could confirm with certainty.

Later, on 30 April, and with the help of aircraft flying from the Task Force itself, the Zone was altered to become a sea and air or Total Exclusion Zone (TEZ), excluding all Argentine aircraft and ships. The next day this aspect was given parallel support by a remarkable raid by a Vulcan bomber of the RAF on Stanley airfield. This aircraft, flying via Ascension Island, four thousand miles away and requiring no less than seven in–flight refuellings, was able to put a large bomb in the middle of the runway. This did not put the airfield out of action completely for planes like the C–130 Hercules, with a short take–off and landing capability, but it did prevent its subsequent use by high performance aircraft such as the Super Etendards. It therefore reduced the threat to our Task Force and enhanced the effectiveness of the Exclusion Zone. It also demonstrated the reach of our attacking aircraft – a point not lost on Buenos Aires.

Paratroops depart on the first stage of their journey to the South Atlantic.
Soldier: Magazine of the British Army

This strategy of heralding our presence round the Falklands by declaring a TEZ not only struck a proper balance between, on the one hand, giving our ships protection and, on the other, not escalating hostilities to too high a level, but it also seized the initiative from the Argentines in a most subtle and admirable manner. Either the Argentines, in order to maintain their naval force in the area of the Falklands, had from then on to run the very great risk that they would be sunk by Britain's powerful nuclear submarines which they could not match, or they had to accept the terms laid down, and be seen to be driven from the seas around the very islands they had claimed as their own, with the consequent loss of face and prestige.

With South Georgia, the Chiefs of Staff deliberations revolved around exactly when it should be recaptured, and the level of force which would be necessary to achieve the aim with the minimum casualties. With its very small garrison, even allowing for some possible reinforcement, and cut off as it was from Argentine air support, South Georgia offered an

excellent opportunity to achieve an early psychological ascendancy over the Argentines, and to set the tone for subsequent operations. This, however, depended on the operation to recapture it being totally and speedily successful; and yet the provision of an adequate force, without excessively weakening or slowing up the main Task Force heading for the Falklands themselves, provided some problems. The Navy had already made some provision to divert a small number of ships under the command of HMS *Antrim* with one company of Royal Marines embarked, and were unwilling to change these arrangements at the last moment. The Army, however, did not think that this size of landing force would necessarily be sufficient to put the issue beyond doubt. Happily the matter was soon resolved by the discovery that D Squadron, SAS (Special Air Service) had got themselves embarked on to the *Antrim* group and were ready for the fray. With these two company–size groups, amounting to over 200 exceptionally fit and highly skilled men, the Chiefs of Staff were satisfied that the operation could go ahead with confidence. The CDS, therefore, after getting the War Cabinet's agreement, ordered the C–in–C to go ahead with the repossession of South Georgia as soon as possible and with the minimum casualties on both sides.

This he did extremely skilfully on 25 April and without any casualties, although the encounter was not without incident and provided a good test of nerve for all concerned. As the *Antrim* group approached South Georgia, the weather became atrocious with visibility down to zero; and, in the process of inserting and subsequently evacuating some SAS reconnaissance parties which had landed before the main assault in order to pin–point the enemy positions, two helicopters crashed. It was only the superb flying by the naval pilot of a third helicopter which averted disaster, by recovering the crew and passengers of both the other two without any loss of life.

But after this disappointing early news – the first of the campaign – fortune suddenly smiled. The weather moderated and the Argentine submarine *Santa Fé*, intending to bring support and some 40 reinforcements to the garrison, was caught on the surface just short of its destination – the anchorage at Grytviken – and disabled by missiles and machine guns. Although it continued to limp into harbour, it was not capable of any serious resistance and the Captain of the *Antrim*, with the enthusiastic encouragement of his embarked troops, seized the opportunity, supported by a covering fire plan which was intended more to frighten than to kill, to follow the submarine in and overwhelm the garrison before they could organize themselves. There was no resistance at all, and indeed the Argentines surrendered before our Special Forces came within small arms range. So within a couple of hours the Union flag was once again run up at Grytviken and later at Leith – the other settlement where it had all started with the arrival of the scrap merchants some five weeks before. Britain had scored the all–important 'opening goal'.

But now, in the last few days of April, Britain was moving literally into altogether more difficult and troubled waters. The first few moves had taken place in a phased approach, allowing plenty of time for political negotiations; the sail south (Phase 1), the recovery of South Georgia (Phase 2), the establishment of the Exclusion Zone and the subsequent bombing of Stanley airfield (Phase 3), and the positioning of our Task Force within striking distance of the TEZ and the Falkland Islands, but out of the most effective operational range of the Argentine Air Force. These had all been predictable, the risks calculated, and success certain. The Chiefs of Staff had all been confident that they would work up to this point, and they did. But as the Task Force came nearer to the Islands themselves (Phase 4) and thus in range of shore–based aircraft and coastal submarines, and with the

very real prospect that, in the absence of any successful negotiations we would actually have to fight to repossess the Islands, the risks grew manifestly higher and the uncertainty greater. In fact, the risks were very high indeed, for the Task Force was still greatly inferior in the air, with less than 40 Sea Harriers operating from two decks in the uncertain weather of the South Atlantic to take on over 200 planes of a front–line mainland–based Argentine Air Force and naval aircraft; a favourable air situation would normally have been an essential precondition of such an operation. Moreover, if anyone still had any doubts about whether both sides were in earnest, and whether lives would have to be lost before matters could be resolved, they were quickly dispelled by the closely linked sinkings of the *Belgrano* and HMS *Sheffield*.

These two incidents highlighted only too clearly the serious state of affairs which had been brought about by the Argentines' initial aggression, and also the further and tragic loss of life which would now have to be expected on

Queen Elizabeth II, carrying 5 Infantry Brigade, leaving Southampton on 12 May. *The Echo*, Southampton

both sides if, despite warnings not only about the TEZ but also about the right of our own ships to protect themselves, the Argentines were still to refuse to evacuate their forces from the Islands.

In effect, of course, while convincing everyone at home that hostilities had already started, and that British forces in the South

Atlantic were not just engaged in some rather ritual demonstration but really meant business and were prepared to do what was necessary, the sinking of the *Belgrano* made a really major contribution towards ensuring that the Argentine Navy never subsequently ventured to sea. This, in turn, contributed to the greater safety of the landing force and the success of the whole operation. However, the sinking also, however justified, as it was, on the grounds of self–defence, made considerable inroads into the fund of goodwill and moral support which had hitherto existed in the international community, and showed what a fine distinction existed between doing what was necessary to achieve military aims and protect our forces and not escalating the war to an extent which could not be sustained in the face of international and perhaps later national criticism. The *Belgrano* sinking also occurred, rather awkwardly for the United States, just after the time when, despite the pro–South America lobby in the State Department, the President and his Secretary of State had made it clear that they were moving from a neutral stance to one which was more supportive of Britain's necessary and unavoidable action, and were now 'tilting for Britain'. It was to their credit that they did not allow the incident to divert them from this in any way.

In any case, whatever criticism there was at the time was soon muted and balanced as a result of the Argentine attack, two days later, by a Super Etendard aircraft using an Exocet missile against HMS *Sheffield*, which was so badly damaged in the attack, while acting as a picket ship to the Task Force steaming north–east of the Falklands, that she later sank. Casualties, including at least 20 dead, were thankfully lighter than might have been expected, but since she was the first Royal Naval ship ever to be crippled and sunk by a remotely–fired missile, it brought home to this country, as nothing else could have done, that our forces in the South Atlantic would from now on be fighting for their lives.

So, with the surface ships of the Task Force now manifestly in action, and the various attempts by General Haig, the United States and later Peru to achieve an acceptable negotiated settlement all foundering, the Chiefs of Staff were now faced with the major problem of the whole campaign: how to repossess the Islands by force. The British people were in no mood for anything which could be interpreted as a 'sell out' or, in view of the publicity attached to the sailing of the Task Force in the first place, as a humiliation for Great Britain, with all the untold consequences for her future credibility in NATO and the World. General Galtieri (the Argentine President) and his junta were in a similar position. There appeared, therefore, in the absence of any acceptable negotiated solution, to be little alternative but to take the plunge and, in view of the tactical balance, to take some calculated risks.

The arguments and counter arguments of the military options were properly debated by the Chiefs of Staff at their daily meetings, and at other more informal gatherings. Indeed it was right and helpful, at a time when the balance of advantage and disadvantage *vis–a–vis* the Argentines was such a fine one and so capable of different interpretations, that there should have been differing shades of opinion, not so much to muddy the advice that would ultimately be given and certainly not to weaken resolve once the die was cast, but to put opportunities and dangers in perspective and to avoid any risk of over–simplifications.

All were agreed that a blockade without an invasion, with all the stress and strain of keeping the Task Force on station throughout the South Atlantic winter, together with the need to send embarked troops back to calmer waters – certainly to South Georgia and probably even as far afield as Ascension Island – was really ruled out as a viable course of action. Moreover, it was clear that, were a blockade policy to be adopted, even accompanied by raids and other minor forms of offensive ac-

Royal Marines line up for a weapons check on the hangar deck of HMS *Hermes*. In the background are Sea Harriers and Sea King helicopters. *Press Association*

tion, it would not only cause immense problems for the morale of the Task Force and Britain's commitments to NATO, but would almost certainly have precipitated a complete falling away in the considerable national and international support we were still enjoying.

There was still, however, the major question to be resolved as to exactly where, when, and in what strength the actual landing should take place, and what sort of preliminary operations should be necessary. With this in mind, Admiral Fieldhouse had been tasked with making, in conjunction with Woodward and Moore, a comprehensive plan to establish a bridgehead on the Falklands with a view to the eventual total repossession of the Islands; this plan was to be presented to the War Cabinet through the Chiefs of Staff. In fact, Fieldhouse had already done much of the outline planning with his subordinate commanders at a meeting held on HMS *Hermes* off Ascension Island as far back as 18 April, and it was only necessary to put the final gloss and detail using up–to–date reconnaissance and intelligence.

When completed, the plan turned out to be both subtle and sensible, and brought back shades of Wolfe's St Lawrence River expedition to Quebec 223 years earlier. In the light of up–to–date information, it was specifically designed to use the sheltered harbour of San Carlos on the west side of East Falkland in order to reduce to a minimum the risks to the amphibious force and its escorts from both air–launched missiles and any submarine that might appear. The plan incorporated preliminary SAS and SBS (Special Boat Squadron) raids to pin–point enemy dispositions, attack targets of opportunity, such as the brilliant raid on the Pucara ground–attack aircraft on Pebble Island, which took place on 15 May, and generally to keep the initiative.

The plan also envisaged creating diversions for over a week, as well as just prior to the landing itself, to distract the enemy from the main effort. For his plan, however, Admiral Fieldhouse required, in addition to the Commando Brigade (now with the Task Force and strengthened to the tune of two parachute battalions, as well as its own three Commandos), a proper reserve, of brigade size, which could be used for a variety of tasks, such as taking over the bridgehead to allow the Commando Brigade to develop its own operations further, or supplementing and reinforcing the Commando Brigade for a two–brigade assault on the capital, Stanley, or even just acting as the new garrison of the Islands, if the Commando Brigade had been able to effect repossession unaided.

But however it might be required to be used, it would be no good having it in the United Kingdom where, even at this early stage, it would be too far away to be considered to be of any value. A reserve, therefore, had to be assembled, given concentrated training and then dispatched in as much comfort and with as much speed as possible, in order to see that Fieldhouse and Woodward could meet their optimum date for the landing which, for a number of reasons, could not be before 16 May and not after the 23rd, and could call on the reserve the moment they needed it.

The first two requirements were complicated by the fact that 5 Brigade – the appropriate Strategic Reserve – had already been denuded of its two parachute battalions to join the Commandos, one of them already 'Spearhead Battalion' and the other 'in role' of a parachute battalion. The Army, therefore, in addition to retaining 5 Brigade's third, Gurkha, battalion

Weapons training, as well as fitness training, regularly took place on deck whilst on passage to the South Atlantic. *Airborne Forces Museum*

in the face of some argument with the Foreign Office, had to select two completely new battalions which would be given a crash course of training to bring them to peak form for the very exacting conditions they would be facing. This was particularly important because, although the two battalions selected, the 2nd Battalion Scots Guards and the 1st Battalion Welsh Guards, were admirable and self–selecting in every other respect (both were first–class battalions and one had only just completed a most successful tour of duty in Northern Ireland), they were at that precise moment on public duties in London and therefore badly and urgently in need of a concentrated period in the field to bring them up to a training peak.

This need for training equally applied to the headquarters of 5 Brigade which, because of financial and manpower cuts, had only been in embryo form and had never previously been exercised on this scale. It soon became clear that the only way that this concentrated training could be achieved and the whole force dispatched to the South Atlantic to arrive in time to support Admiral Fieldhouse's plan was to requisition the great passenger liner, the *Queen Elizabeth II*, and send the whole reserve force in her in one lift.

In the various discussions which took place inside the Chiefs of Staff Committee and between the CDS and Fleet Headquarters, and before framing firm advice to Ministers, the General Staff had been initially unhappy that the landing site proposed by Fieldhouse was so far away from the ultimate objectives at Stanley and would, therefore, involve a lengthy and exhausting cross–country movement before the key high ground west of Stanley could be properly invested and attacked. This, they felt, would run the considerable risk that, if Argentine resistance was at all dynamic, the infantry might get stuck half–way across East Falkland with the winter settling in, and perhaps with increasing international pressure to agree to a totally unsatisfactory and inconclusive cease–

fire as well. But I, as CGS, soon became personally convinced that nothing must be done to make the landing areas, landing sites and ships standing–by near them, more vulnerable to the sea–skimming air to surface missiles. For this would be when the Task Force was most vulnerable while, once ashore, the risk of an attack on the land forces would recede quickly and they would then be able to exert their professionalism over the Argentine conscripts. The distance from Stanley would have to be accepted. Admiral Fieldhouse's plan, therefore, had the unanimous backing of the Chiefs when it was presented to the War Cabinet and subsequently approved by them, subject always to no satisfactory negotiations becoming possible.

Once the reserve brigade was within striking distance, and with the negotiations accepted by the War Cabinet to have virtually broken down, the final decision by the Government could and indeed had to be taken if Woodward was to effect his ship redeployment in time for a landing a few days later and meet his 'window of opportunity'. For this decision all the Chiefs, together with the War Cabinet, were assembled in the Cabinet Room at Downing Street on 19 May and each in turn was required to back his own judgement and say how he saw any landing turning out and whether it should be attempted. Even in hindsight it is doubtful if any would have wished to change the views they expressed, but in any event the options before us were not that many. For the problem all along had been that no solution – military or negotiated – was possible unless the Task Force sailed, and at the time it did, no one could really be sure whether military repossession was feasible or not. Yet once the Task Force had reached its destination, the repercussions of sailing it all the way back again having achieved nothing (other than South Georgia) were so great that military opinion would have had to have been absolutely certain that an attempt to repossess by force would be bound to

fail, before advising against it; and the odds were far too finely balanced to be able to do that.

So the die was cast. By dint of heroism, skill, and quick learning on the part of the Royal Navy, careful selection of the weather and use of the configuration of the hills and coastline in San Carlos Sound to keep the vulnerability of the ships to the minimum, and by taking the calculated risk also of bringing the converted cruise liner SS *Canberra* into the Sound as well as the assault ships *Fearless* and *Intrepid*, the operation went ahead with commendable smoothness. Nearly 5,000 men were landed with scarcely any casualties, and this was to be repeated in the same place, some seven to ten days later, with the whole of 5 Infantry Brigade.

It was a great triumph for Admiral Woodward who had handled his Task Force with consummate skill throughout. The consequent losses, however, once the Argentines reacted, were, as had been anticipated, quite high and might have been higher still. Five ships were lost in the aftermath of the landing, or during the course of the subsequent three–week battle, and ten others were damaged, mostly through unexploded bombs. 34 aircraft, fixed wing and helicopters, were also to be lost, and over 115 Army and Royal Marines were killed in the subsequent fighting around Goose Green and in the mountains west of Stanley before victory was won, including about 50 in the air attack on the logistic ship *Sir Galahad* with the Welsh Guards on board.

But despite these set–backs, including the loss of the *Atlantic Conveyor* containing valuable helicopters and stores, the most difficult part of the whole operation had, with the landing, been successfully completed and the way to Stanley was now open if the opportunities could be grasped. In the process of grasping them, the Task Force would manage to put out of action virtually 80% of the Argentine air forces, which fought bravely, and thus to achieve the sort of favourable or tolerable air situation which had not been possible prior to

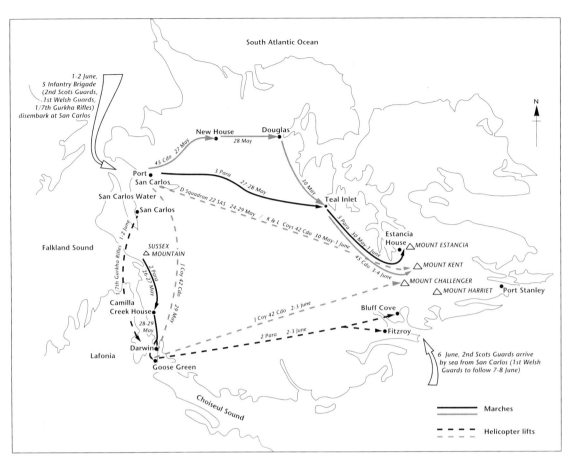

The advance of the British Forces, 24 May to 6 June

the landing itself. The Argentine Navy, moreover, after the sinking of the *Belgrano*, had remained skulking within 12 nautical miles of its coastline, and played no further part in the campaign.

Immediately after the Commando Brigade had established the bridgehead, there was a tactical hiatus, bred both from an acute shortage of helicopters, which had slowed down the logistic build–up, and also from some misunderstanding by the Brigade of its tasks and objectives; and the absence of Moore for the first crucial days had contributed to this. Minds in the UK, therefore, inevitably went back to many landings in military history which had floundered because, after a successful assault, the opportunity had not been taken to exploit while the going was good. The risk of getting stuck half–way across East Falkland by weather could still be a strong possibility and this was perhaps an example of how, with the help of the wider intelligence picture held in Whitehall,

the tactical dangers and opportunities could be seen rather more clearly 8,000 miles away in London, than they were on the spot.

However, once the decision had been taken to move out of the bridgehead, first to Goose Green and then on to Stanley, the excellent and powerful Commando Brigade got under way with great style and physical toughness. The position was then suddenly transformed in our favour by the heroic action of 2 Para at Goose Green who, taking on what turned out to be quite three times their number, secured an objective of great depth and much complexity, taking about a thousand prisoners.

It was an operation that can well compare with the epics of military history and it certainly reflected the greatest credit on the whole Battalion, its motivation and its training, particularly by Lieutenant–Colonel 'H' Jones, the Commanding Officer, who tragically lost his life in heroic circumstances and was to be posthumously awarded the Victoria Cross.

By the end of the first week of June, General Moore had two full brigades ashore, consisting of eight battalions, large numbers of helicopters, five batteries of artillery with adequate ammunition, air defence (Rapier and Blowpipe), and was still supported by Harriers and naval gunpower. Despite the unlucky setback of the *Sir Galahad* during the bringing forward of the Welsh Guards to Bluff Cove, which had to be done by sea because there were insufficient helicopters, the enemy had been compressed into a small area round Stanley, and Moore dominated him from the high ground to the west. So there was now no possible reason why British forces should fail to repossess the Islands. The important thing was for commanders on the spot to ensure that full use was made of such fire support as was available, and that there was proper co–ordination of fire and movement which could progressively and methodically make the Argentine positions around Stanley untenable, and force them to surrender.

And this is exactly what happened. 42 and 45 Commandos, in a superb night attack, helped undoubtedly by the withholding of casualty details at Bluff Cove (because the Argentines, it was subsequently learned, thought British casualties were far greater than they were and expected the attack to be delayed at least two weeks), captured Two Sisters and Mount Harriet, and 3 Para, after a tough fight rivalling 2 Para's at Goose Green, seized Mount Longdon. The total casualties along the front for this second phase were 21 dead and about 70 to 80 wounded. The next phase, in which 2 Para, benefitting from their experience at Goose Green, attacked Wireless Hill, immediately north–west of Stanley, the Scots Guards went for the Tumbledown feature held by the Argentine marines, and the 1/7th (Duke of Edinburgh's Own) Gurkha Rifles attacked Mount William, all of which were expected to be the really tough positions to crack, was completed with remarkably few casualties – only six killed and 17 wounded in all three operations. Once this had been achieved, the whole Argentine position collapsed. Indeed the Gurkhas, with their formidable reputation no doubt preceding them, hardly had to fight for Mount William at

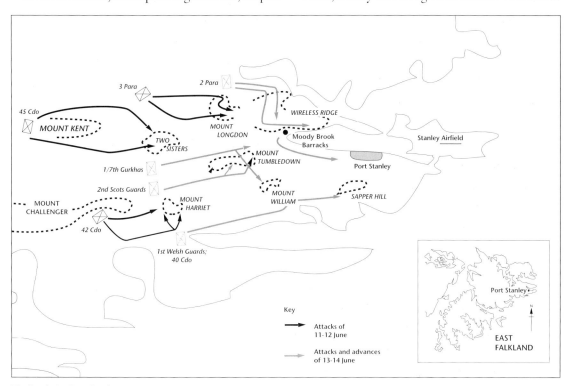

The battle for Port Stanley

all. As they approached, the Argentines just turned and fled into Stanley, taking the next position in depth, Sapper Hill, with them. And in the follow–up, 2 Para, 45 Commando, and the Welsh Guards merely had to walk into Stanley with the Argentines surrendering and throwing down their arms all round them. A final total of prisoners on the Falkland Islands was to be about 11,000, mostly in Stanley, instead of the 6,000 to 7,000 which it was believed were there at the time.

History will no doubt look back with admiration on what, under any circumstances, and against a far from inept enemy, was a triumphant feat of arms, with excellent inter–Service co–operation. For this the principal credit must go to the courage, toughness and professionalism of the commanders and men on the spot and to the efficiency and dedication of the logistic chain the whole way down the line.

Although the total casualties of 255 from all three Services killed and 775 wounded was

a matter of the greatest regret and grief, the operation, apart from restoring legitimate rule in the face of aggression, did prove to have done an enormous amount for Britain's status and the respect shown for her in the causes of peace and of making the world safer for others.

If it looked like a close–run thing, well, perhaps the best epitaph for this small but highly significant episode in British history might be taken from a passage from one of Winston Churchill's World War II speeches, in which he said that 'All great struggles in history have been won by superior willpower wresting victory in the face of odds or upon the narrowest of margins.' For the greatest single factor in the Falklands campaign was undoubt-edly that all ranks of all three Services showed the will to take the risks, the will to overcome the obstacles, the will to face dangers and the will, if need be, to make the final sacrifice, the will to decide and the will to win – the indomi-table spirit of the Warrior.

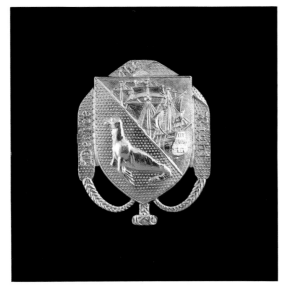 

Badge commemorating the part played by the Falkland Islands Volunteer Corps in the defence of the Islands, 1914.
Awarded to Private Robert Montgomery. *National Army Museum 8207–33*

The Land Battle

Major–General Julian Thompson (Brigade Commander, 3 Commando Brigade, Falklands War)

The land battle was the key to winning the Falklands War. Only by defeating the Argentine Army and seizing the strategic objective, Port Stanley, could Britain achieve her aim of repossessing the Falkland Islands.

Before these goals could be attained, British troops had to be landed on the Falkland Islands. The question was where? The commander's aim in any amphibious operation is to build up his forces as fast as possible, and then advance to seize his objectives. This will be impossible if the enemy attacks in strength by land, sea or air, at an early stage, before the landing force holds a sizeable area into which the commander can land sufficient men, guns, helicopters, and supplies to engage the enemy with a chance of defeating him.

The landing force commander also has to take account of the needs of the navy, who are responsible for: landing him and his supplies in the right place, supporting him with landing craft, helicopters, naval gunfire, and protecting the shipping and amphibious operating area against attack by submarine, surface ships and aircraft. The selection of the beach–head, and the timing and method of landing, are decided jointly by the landing force commander and the amphibious group commander.

The commanders responsible for making these decisions were Brigadier Julian Thompson, commanding 3 Commando Brigade Royal Marines, and Commodore Michael Clapp, commanding all amphibious ships, including civilian ships taken up from trade (STUFT) and escorts. 3 Commando Brigade, consisting of numbers 40, 42, and 45 Commando Royal Marines, 29 Commando Regiment Royal Artillery, and 59 Commando Squadron Royal Engineers, and other supporting units, had been reinforced by the 2nd and 3rd Battalions The Parachute Regiment.

Thompson and Clapp chose San Carlos, which met most of their requirements. Most important for Thompson, it was far enough away from the Argentine main positions around Port Stanley to enable the build–up to proceed without early interference by Argentine ground forces. This was vital, bearing in mind how few helicopters were available, so most ship–shore movements would have to be by slow and vulnerable landing craft. The main disadvantage was the distance to Port Stanley, 50 miles in a straight line, the equivalent of London to Brighton.

Terrain and climate are always an important consideration when planning a land campaign. In East Falkland most of the terrain consists of peat bog with, in places, large areas of hummocky tussock grass. Except for a few stunted growths in the settlements, there are no trees at all. In daylight, and in good weather, movement on the open hillsides, devoid of cover, can be seen for miles in the clear unpolluted air. Stone runs abound, up to hundreds of yards wide and several miles long, like rivers of stone consisting of boulders varying from the size of a coconut to that of a car. Moving across stone runs by day was painfully slow. At night the stones clinked and men slipped on the greasy lichen.

The mountains, although not high, and more akin to moorland hills (the highest, Mount Usborne, being 2,300 feet), were almost all covered with great, craggy castles of rock, standing up like the spines of some vast prehistoric reptile. These crenellated bastions, with deep fissures, sudden sheer drops, and great buttresses were obstacles to any type of vehicle, wheeled or tracked. Few were less than 500 yards long, and some in excess of 2,000.

In 1982, apart from the environs of Stanley, and an unsurfaced track to Fitzroy, there were no roads or tracks. A lightly–loaded Landrover would be lucky to cover four miles in the hour,

2 Para on board *Norland* waiting for the assault to begin, 21 May. *Airborne Forces Museum*

provided it kept off tussock and stone run, and did not follow the tracks of a predecessor which had broken through the light crust and reduced the going to a black slurry. A wheeled vehicle loaded with ammunition or towing a gun would not move at all. 3 Commando Brigade took 76 of its BV 202 (Bandwagons), tracked oversnow vehicles, the remainder were stockpiled in Norway. It was assessed that Bandwagons, with a ground pressure equivalent to a man on skis, would cope with the peat bog.

The only other vehicles with the Brigade capable of moving across the country were the four Scimitar and four Scorpion (Combat Vehicle Reconnaissance Tracked (CVRT)), and the light armoured recovery vehicle, of the Blues and Royals (RHG/D).

Although the Falklands lie on the same latitude south of the equator as Britain does north, the great Southern Ocean, with no equivalent of the Gulf Stream to warm the sea, and the proximity of the vast frozen continent of Antarctica, Cape Horn and the Andes, combine to make the climate significantly different. Icebergs regularly come within 200 miles of the Islands. Snow, rain, fog, and brilliant sunshine follow each other with bewildering rapidity at all times of the year, even in summer; the land battles were fought in the month leading up to midwinter. The only constant is the wind; the average windspeed throughout the year in Britain is four knots, in the Falklands it is 16 knots (18.5 mph).

The harsh terrain, uncompromising weather, lack of roads and paucity of helicopters shaped this war. The almost total lack of cover and warmth away from the settlements meant that once a man was wet, he usually stayed wet; the best that could be achieved was a state of clammy dampness. Most men's feet never dried and many suffered from trench–foot. Living day and night in peat or rock–walled sangars, where the shallowest scrape filled with water within minutes, was far from pleasant. Ammunition took absolute priority over everything in the competition for helicopters flying forward, as did casualties on the return trips. Units were often short of food. Perversely, in this sodden land, water was difficult to find except in a few valley bottoms. Shallow pits in the peat yielded a brackish brew. Puritabs sterilized, but did not remove the sediment which inflamed the gut. As the land war progressed, many suffered 'Galtieri's Revenge'. To avoid unnecessary delay disrobing, some men dispensed with underpants, and cut a slit in the seat of their trousers. On the march and in battle, troops of all arms carried heavy loads. For the marines and soldiers, it was a low–tech war; marching, patrolling, freezing days and nights, savage gutter fighting, foot soldiers closing with the enemy, primitive, unforgiving.

By 13 May, when Thompson gave his orders to his brigade for the landing at San Carlos, it was clear that the Argentines had about 11,000 troops on the Falkland Islands. Reports from Special Forces patrols and other intelligence sources had enabled the brigade intelligence staff to build up a good outline picture of the forces round Stanley. Except for detailed locations, especially gun positions, most of what was actually there had been identified: a reinforced brigade consisting of six infantry regiments (each battalion size), including a marine unit, a comprehensive gun and surface–to–air (SAM) air defence system, supporting arms and logistic units. The artillery supporting this brigade consisted of 38 105mm pack howitzers with a range of 10km, and three towed 155mm guns with a range of 24km. In addition there were numerous 35mm and 30mm air defence guns, which the Argentines also used in the ground role.

Intelligence had been less forthcoming about the enemy strength at Darwin and Goose Green. Assessments varied from a reinforced company, the original garrison, to a weak battalion plus air force personnel to man the airstrip, some artillery and air defence. The second estimate was nearer the truth. Of the total garrison strength of 1,500, the Argentines had 554 infantry (a mixed bag made up from three different regiments) three 105mm pack howitzers, plus some 30mm air defence guns. Of the total garrison, nearly 1,000 were from the air force.

A brigade of two infantry regiments (battalions) with artillery and air defence garrisoned West Falkland. Most of the 34 airstrips on the Islands had been assessed as capable of operating Pucaras, Aermacchis, and other light aircraft; some could accept C–130s. What was being used, and for what, was never clear right up to the end of the war. One set of clear air photographs would have helped answer this and a host of other questions about the enemy. Contrary to rumour, there was never any friendly satellite coverage of the Falklands, or if there was, none of its intelligence, if any, was made available to those who could have used it.

By the start of the campaign, the force around Stanley alone outnumbered 3 Commando Brigade, had more guns, more helicopters, air superiority, and the added bonus of T34C Mentors, Pucaras, Aermacchi M339s, and Augusta Bell 109A Attack Helicopters positioned in the Islands. The British had declared a maritime and air blockade, but during the day Argentine fighters were able to penetrate to the Islands and carry out attacks. The

3 Para goes ashore from landing craft at San Carlos soon after dawn, 21 May. *Airborne Forces Museum*

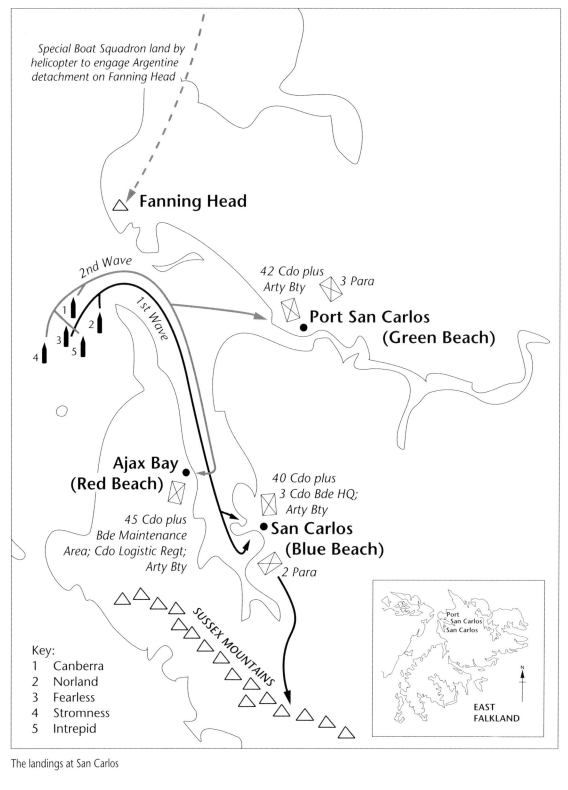

Key:
1 Canberra
2 Norland
3 Fearless
4 Stromness
5 Intrepid

The landings at San Carlos

Argentines flew C–130s into the strip at Port Stanley up to the last night of the war.

The landings, starting just after midnight on 21 May 1982, took longer than anticipated, mainly because of the Argentine air attacks, which started about two hours after first light, and, except for a break on D+1 (22 May), persisted for the next six days. Clapp and Thompson had been promised air superiority over the beach–head. However, it was not achieved, and the landings had to proceed without one of the usual pre–requisites for such an operation.

By midday the Brigade had seized all its D–Day objectives, and dug–in to defend the

beach–head while guns, ammunition, and supplies were landed. Two of the Brigade's Gazelle helicopters had been shot down by the
small Argentine garrison of Port San Carlos
(three aircrew killed and one wounded). A
half–company of Argentines on Fanning Head
had been killed, captured, or had run away.
However, Thompson's plan to keep most of
his supplies and much of his medical support
loaded in ships ready to move round to support
his advance across East Falkland, had to be
modified in the face of the Argentine air attacks. For the next six days, the helicopters and
landing craft were engaged in the logistic
offload. The Advanced Dressing Station and
one surgical team, as well as the Parachute
Clearing Troop, were installed in the disused
mutton processing factory at Ajax Bay.

The problem now was to move the Brigade to the high ground overlooking Port
Stanley. Well before landing, Thompson had
planned to fly the bulk of his brigade to Mount
Kent and the adjacent features; once the five
Chinook heavy–lift and six Wessex medium–
lift helicopters had arrived on the container
ship *Atlantic Conveyor*. These, with the eleven
Sea King and five Wessex medium–lift helicopters already in the beach–head, would be
just sufficient to make the operation feasible.
Once established on the Mount Kent feature,
Landing Ships Logistics (LSLs) could enter
Port Salvador to unload at Teal Inlet. From
here supplies could be flown forward by helicopter; considerably shorter than the trip from
the San Carlos beach–head. Thompson had
discarded any approach from the south and the
south–west. He believed that the Argentines
expected the main assault would come from
that direction. Subsequent intelligence con
firmed this view, and we now know that the
enemy defences were orientated to counter
such an attack.

By D–Day, Thompson had not decided
on the timing of the forward move of the
Brigade. Before landing he had been sent a

directive by Major–General Moore, who was
coming south with the Divisional Headquarters and 5 Infantry Brigade. It read:

*You are to secure a bridgehead on East Falkland,
into which reinforcements can be landed, in
which an airstrip can be established and from
which operations to repossess the Falklands can
be achieved.*

*You are to push forward from the bridge-
head area so far as the maintenance of its security
allows, to gain information, to establish moral
and physical domination over the enemy, and to
forward the ultimate objective of repossession.
You will retain operational control of all forces
landed in the Falklands until I establish my
Headquarters in the area. It is my intention to
do this, aboard* Fearless, *as early as practicable
after the landings. I expect this to be approximately on D+7. It is then my intention to land
5 Infantry Brigade into the beachhead and to
develop operations for the complete repossession
of the Falkland Islands.*

Thompson took this to mean that he was to
hold the beach–head, while probing out, and in
particular pushing reconnaissance teams forward to find suitable helicopter landing zones
near Mount Kent, place observation posts on
the high ground overlooking the route from
San Carlos to Mount Kent, and provide reception parties at Teal Inlet. This he proceeded to
do, starting on the evening of D–Day, having
made it clear in his orders that the landing was
only a beginning and not an end in itself. While
it was possible that he might fly some of his
brigade forward, it was not his understanding
that he could move all units out of the beach–
head until the arrival of 5 Infantry Brigade and
Divisional Headquarters.

Until the logistic offload had been completed, and more helicopters had arrived, advancing to the high ground overlooking Stanley
would be foolhardy. The infantry could advance on foot, but major battles, or repelling

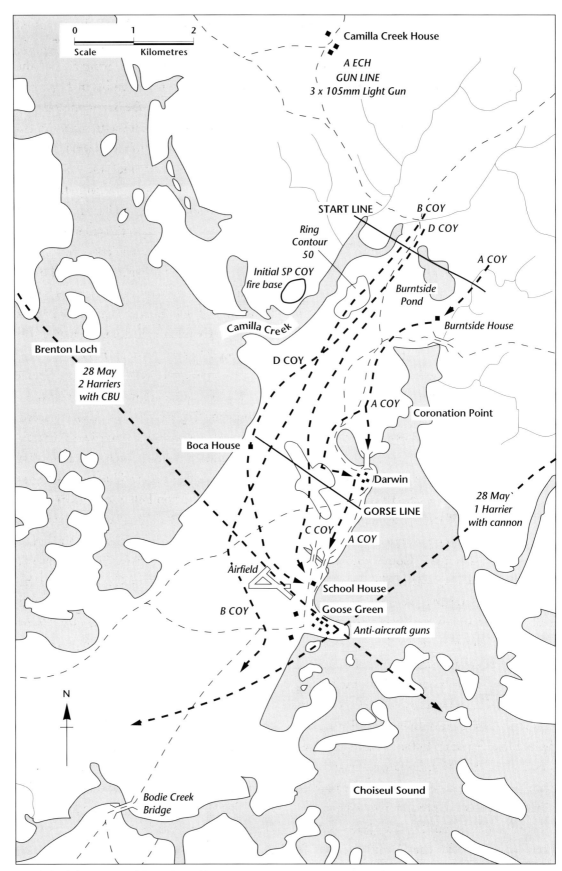

2 Para's battle for Darwin and Goose Green, 28 May

counter–attacks on the key positions near Stanley, would require heavy ammunition expenditure–shells and mortar bombs in particular. The only way to lift these was by helicopter, and there were insufficient helicopters to maintain a substantial force in contact with the enemy over the distances involved.

However, all this was to change as pressure built up at home for a move out of the beach–head. Thompson was unable to discuss this with Moore, who, travelling from Ascension in the liner *Queen Elizabeth II*, found himself unable to communicate with the beach–head. On 25 May, Thompson was ordered to start the move. He and his staff were putting the finishing touches to the plan, which relied on the Chinooks arriving at San Carlos in *Atlantic Conveyor* the following morning, when a staff officer informed them that the ship had been sunk by an air–launched Exocet. All but one Chinook and every Wessex helicopter had gone with her.

At first, Thompson's reaction was to sit tight until Moore arrived. However, Admiral Fieldhouse, the Task Force commander at Northwood, summoned him to the satellite telephone to say that 3 Commando Brigade was to start moving out of the beach–head. Furthermore, an attack on Goose Green, originally planned as a raid and subsequently cancelled by Thompson, was to be remounted.

Thompson ordered Lieutenant–Colonel Whitehead, commanding 45 Commando, and Lieutenant–Colonel Pike, commanding 3 Para, to march to Teal Inlet, where a patrol from the Special Boat Squadron (SBS) was already in hiding. Lieutenant–Colonel Jones, commanding 2 Para, was ordered to take the twin settlements of Darwin and Goose Green, and hold them.

At last light on 26 May, Jones led his battalion south off Sussex Mountain towards Camilla Creek House. Soon after first light on the 27th, 45 Commando and 3 Para set off for Teal Inlet, 45 Commando having been told to march via Douglas Settlement.

At 0250 hrs on 28 May 2 Para crossed their start line, and the long battle for Darwin and Goose Green began. Having cleared the forward positions, occupied by an Argentine company, by first light, the Battalion closed up to what soon became clear was the enemy main position. This roughly followed what the Battalion called the 'gorse line', stretching from Boca House in the west to Darwin Hill in the east. The momentum of the Battalion's attack ground to a halt, and casualties mounted. Dead and wounded parachute soldiers were stripped of their ammunition. Soldiers armed with Sterling sub–machine–guns, useless in most situations, threw them away, and picked up SLRs from the wounded and dead, or better still Argentine FALs which fired in bursts.

In an attempt to break the deadlock, Jones was mortally wounded leading an assault on the Darwin Hill position. He was later awarded the Victoria Cross, posthumously. Eventually using 66mm anti–tank rocket launchers to blast the Argentine trenches and bunkers, A Company cleared Darwin Hill in a series of close–quarter battles. 'The Toms just put their heads down and went for it', said one officer later.

On the western flank, Major Crosland managed to pull back his B Company from the forward slopes, and engage Boca House with Milan wire–guided anti–tank missiles. Major Neame led his D Company, crawling along the beach behind a tiny shelf, to take the Boca House positions in the flank.

Just after midday, Major Keeble, the second–in–command, ordered the Battalion to advance to Goose Green, securing the airstrip en route. As the afternoon wore on, the Battalion fought its way down and across the isthmus. The fighting was tough as the Argentines fought tenaciously and subjected the attackers to artillery fire.

As the Battalion reorganized on a ridgeline overlooking Goose Green, two Argentine Aermacchis from Stanley attacked with rockets and cannon. Both were greeted by a stream of ground fire. Marine Strange of 3 Commando Brigade Air Defence, 'standing up as though in a butt at a grouse drive', shot down one with a Blowpipe missile. Shortly after, two Pucara, one armed with napalm, attacked. One was shot down by small arms fire. The pilot ejected, and was taken prisoner. His aircraft crashed close by, drenching several men with fuel and napalm, which fortunately did not ignite. One man, lying face down, had his back pouches scythed off by part of a wing.

Despite these encouraging successes, 2 Para could make no headway against the anti-aircraft guns on the Goose Green peninsula. They were well out of range of any of the Battalion's weapons, and the supporting artillery had run out of ammunition. As the winter afternoon began to fade, the battle hung in the balance. 2 Para had been fighting for 14 hours, through three and a half miles of defences. At that moment, three Harriers arrived, having been prevented by bad weather at sea from taking part in the battle all day, and, under the control of the Naval Gunfire Support Forward Observer (NGSFO), also a trained Forward Air Controller (FAC), attacked with cluster bombs and cannon. The violent blast of the cluster bombs, 47 to a cluster, rippling like a giant Chinese fire-cracker, silenced the anti-aircraft guns. Civilians released from the settlement the next day reported that the enemy soldiers had sobbed and screamed in terror.

The Argentines at Goose Green were reinforced twice during the battle. At about midday, a weak company was flown in to the south of the settlement in 11 helicopters from Stanley, and ran in to join the garrison. At dusk, about 140 men from the Argentine force reserve located on the lower northern slopes of Mount Kent were landed by helicopter, again south of Goose Green, and joined the garrison after dark.

Thompson ordered 42 Commando to despatch a company to reinforce 2 Para. J Company was sent. Formed to replace M Company, detached to South Georgia, it contained some men who had been part of the Royal Marines detachment when the Argentines invaded eight weeks before.

Just before midday on 29 May, the Argentine garrison, threatened with an air strike and an artillery bombardment, surrendered. 2 Para had fought perhaps the most remarkable single battalion action by the British Army since the Second World War. Other authors have written, and no doubt it will continue to be said, that in 2 Para (as with 3 Para, the Commandos and the Scots Guards), the Argentines were fighting the finest soldiers in the British Army, and therefore among the best in the world, with a largely conscript army. This is true, but laymen may not realise that a man, however inexperienced, dug-in with a machine gun, is at a considerable advantage against several men, however well trained and motivated, advancing in the open. If the attackers are not sure exactly where the opponent is, and lack adequate artillery and mortar support, the situation at Goose Green, they are at an even greater disadvantage. They can only overcome by first-class soldiering, and above all the will to win. The victory by 2 Para, and indeed subsequent victories by other British Commandos and battalions, despite considerably greater fire support than was available at Goose Green, should also be viewed in this light. Attacking troops were never near the 3:1 advantage in numbers called for by the text books; a ratio of 1.5:1 was the average.

There is no doubt that Thompson made three mistakes in this battle, perhaps symptomatic of his belief that it was an unnecessary diversion from the aim of seizing Stanley. First, he should have taken his tactical headquarters, and commanded in person. Second, he should have taken another battalion or Commando with him. Third, he should have taken at least a troop of CVRT. Had he done all three, the battle would have been over far quicker. This is not intended as a criticism of Jones and Keeble. Merely that their Brigade Commander asked more of 2 Para than he should have done. As Crosland commented later, 'it was a come as you are' party.

Perhaps, if he regarded it as a diversion, Thompson made a fourth error, in not refusing to attack Goose Green in the first place. Although in the end good came out of it, this could not have been foreseen, nor the credit claimed, by those who ordered the attack from 8,000 miles away.

This battle was to have a profound effect on the conduct of the rest of the campaign. It signalled to the Argentines the absolute determination of the British to succeed. It opened up the southern route to Stanley, and because the Argentines were convinced almost to the end that the main attack would come from the south–west, perhaps along the axis of the Fitzroy–Stanley track, it served to confirm their perception, distracting them from what was actually the major thrust by 3 Commando Brigade from the north and west. The fighting over the bare slopes in daylight had been costly. From then on the Brigade would if possible fight at night. The confusion of battle in darkness would be offset by the greater skill of the British soldiers and marines, the better leadership, and the intimate and flexible fire support by their magnificent gunners. Finally, and again unforeseen, the Argentine heliborne reserve had been drawn away from the vital area of Mount Kent and taken prisoner with the rest of the Goose Green garrison. They were not, therefore, able to intervene during the highly risky three days, when a light force of 42 Commando and a Special Air Service (SAS) squadron with minimum support was pushed forward on to Mount Kent.

While the battle for Goose Green was under way, 45 Commando and 3 Para were marching to Teal Inlet. An attempt made on the night 29/30 May to fly part of 42 Commando to Mount Kent had to be aborted because of a snow blizzard. D Squadron 22 SAS, had flown in on successive nights to secure a landing zone, starting on the night 24/25 May. The Squadron was finally complete by the night 28/29 May. Taking five nights to fly in one SAS squadron, about 50 men, is indication enough of the frustrations caused by bad weather at night, woefully few helicopters, and the Goose Green diversion.

A soldier of 3 Para seeking information from Islanders after the Battalion had cleared Port San Carlos settlement. *Airborne Forces Museum*

On 30 May General Moore arrived in the beach–head. After hearing what Thompson and his staff had to say, he approved all the moves that had been planned. Thompson greeted his arrival with profound relief. The move forward of 3 Commando Brigade Headquarters could now proceed as planned, without worrying about the need to remain in touch with the Task Force Headquarters at Northwood by satellite telephone. Moore would also assume responsibility for the daily, sometimes more frequent, conversations with Northwood.

Moore told Thompson that 40 Commando, now holding the entire beach–head, would be relieved by a battalion of 5 Infantry Brigade, and move forward to join their own brigade. Thompson warned 40 Commando to be prepared to march to Teal Inlet.

Moore ordered Brigadier Wilson commanding 5 Infantry Brigade to Goose Green, where he was to take command of 2 Para. Wilson had brought with him 2nd Battalion Scots Guards, 1st Battalion Welsh Guards, and 1st Battalion 7th Gurkha Rifles.

Weapons surrendered by Argentine troops at Goose Green, 29 May. *Airborne Forces Museum*

On the night 30/31 May, Tactical Headquarters 42 Commando, K Company, the Mortar Troop, and three 105mm light guns of 7 (Sphinx) Commando Light Battery were flown forward to a landing zone below Mount Kent. By first light on 31 May, K Company was on the summit. The Argentines had committed a major error in not holding this feature strongly. Indeed they had never included it in their defensive layout. The nearest troops were the helicopter reserve, located well down from the summit, and most had gone 48 hours before 42 Commando arrived. D Squadron 22 SAS had several clashes with Argentine 602 Commando Company in the Mount Kent area, an indication that the enemy hoped to cover this and other features with patrols to harass any British advance.

According to one account, 602 Commando Company considered this role beneath them, hoping to operate behind British lines. Judged by their performance on Mount Kent

and elsewhere, despite their undoubted courage, their standards of training were low, only marginally better than the run of the mill Argentine conscripts.

The biggest action by 602 Commando Company occurred when an observation post (OP) of 3 Commando Brigade Reconnaissance Troop provided by the Mountain and Arctic Warfare Cadre, spotted a large enemy patrol occupying Top Malo House. It was important that unfriendly eyes should not overlook 3 Commando Brigade's line of communication from San Carlos–Teal Inlet–Mount Kent, so patrols from the Cadre had been posted on several key features overlooking the route to Mount Kent since the evening of D–Day.

Soon after first light on 31 May, a fighting patrol from the Cadre, under its commander Captain Boswell, was dropped by helicopter in a valley out of sight of Top Malo House. They approached unseen and, after a fierce little battle, killed or captured the entire Argentine patrol. Unknown to Boswell and his men, the assault had been watched by two other 602 Commando Company patrols who, having seen the treatment meted out to their comrades and imagining that it was their turn next, surrendered to the nearest British troops.

By 4 June most of 3 Commando Brigade, less 40 Commando, still back at San Carlos, had deployed forward on the high ground Mount Estancia–Mount Vernet–Mount Kent–Mount Challenger. Despite repeated requests that 40 Commando be released to 3 Commando Brigade, Moore decided to keep them back in the beach–head, having been warned by intelligence from Northwood that the Argentines were planning an airborne assault on the area. This caused considerable bitterness among all ranks, particularly when they saw one of the battalions of 5 Infantry Brigade having difficulty in marching from San Carlos to Goose Green. First–class leadership by the commanding officer, Lieutenant–Colonel Hunt, maintained morale in the face of an order which to this day is still misunderstood by many who served in 40 Commando.

By 3 June, the leading elements of 5 Infantry Brigade, 2 Para, were at Fitzroy and Bluff Cove. This move, far swifter than anticipated, thanks to the initiative of Major Keeble, took Divisional Headquarters by surprise. Having originally allocated the bulk of the helicopter support to 3 Commando Brigade, they were forced to reassign most to 5 Infantry Brigade. Although more helicopters had arrived, the medium and heavy–lift helicopter force remained grossly inadequate to the end of the war.

The remainder of 5 Infantry Brigade moved to the Fitzroy–Bluff Cove area over a series of days and nights. The sea move of 2nd Battalion Scots Guards culminated in a disagreeable trip by landing craft. After a night passage from San Carlos in HMS *Intrepid*, routing south of Lafonia, the intention was to launch the four large landing craft (LCUs), with the Battalion embarked, off Choiseul Sound. This would have entailed a run–in to Bluff Cove of a couple of hours or so, unwelcome enough for even the most experienced troops, in lumpy seas, with spray and snow showers in the pitch blackness. Few, if any, in this Battalion had been in a landing craft before, except for short trips in sheltered waters, in daylight.

Despite protestations by Major Southby–Tailyour, an officer of vast experience in operating landing craft, and with greater knowledge of the waters round the Falklands than anyone in the Task Force, the Captain of *Intrepid* launched the landing craft south–west of Lively Island. *Intrepid* steamed off into the darkness. For seven hours, soaked, shivering and sea–sick, the Guardsmen endured. Southby–Tailyour had only the highest praise for their fortitude, and admiration for their morale in these unfamiliar and daunting surroundings. It was fortunate that he knew these waters so well, because at one stage the radar on his landing craft broke down. At one point the

flotilla of craft was fired at by what Southby–Tailyour thought were mortars or light artillery, although who fired these is a mystery. This was followed by a heart–stopping moment, when HMS *Cardiff*, on the gun–line bombarding the enemy positions round Stanley, challenged and fired star–shell. Admiral Woodward, although appraised of the move to Bluff Cove by Commodore Clapp, had failed to inform the ships on the gun–line that night. Disaster was averted when in reply to *Cardiff*'s challenge 'friend' by signal lamp, Southby–Tailyour, flashed back 'to whom?'

At least the move of 2nd Battalion Scots Guards was not marred by any casualties; 1st Battalion Welsh Guards was not so fortunate. A series of mishaps led to the bombing of LSLs *Sir Galahad* and *Sir Tristram* at Fitzroy on 8 June, with the loss of 43 dead, and over 200 wounded, the majority from 1st Battalion Welsh Guards. Lack of space precludes an analysis of the full story, and apportioning blame is fruitless. The incident must be seen against a background of great haste to move 5 Infantry Brigade forward. But it must be said that a major factor was an order from Northwood forbidding Clapp to send either *Fearless* or *Intrepid* to the south of Fitzroy again. The moral here is that proper command from 8,000 miles away is impossible.

While 5 Infantry Brigade was concentrating around Fitzroy and Bluff Cove, 3 Commando Brigade was patrolling vigorously to obtain information and dominate the enemy. The Brigade plan, submitted to Divisional Headquarters, was to start by seizing three features, Mount Longdon, Two Sisters and Mount Harriet. Once these were taken, Thompson wanted to exploit forward to Mount Tumbledown, Wireless Ridge, and possibly Mount William. With these in his hands, the way to Stanley would be open. Possession of these features ensured that he could maintain his line of communication by helicopter and Bandwagon following the lower ground along

Survivors from the stricken *Sir Galahad* reach the shore at Fitzroy, 8 June. *Airborne Forces Museum*

the line of the Estancia House–Moody Brook track dominated by Mount Longdon, Two Sisters, Tumbledown, and Wireless Ridge. Although a track in name only until about three miles short of Moody Brook, the lower ground, usually mist–free, was the key to ensuring that the flow of ammunition forward, and casualty evacuation rearward, could be maintained day and night, and in almost all weathers. Mount Harriet would provide a firm anchor to his right flank, and, with Two Sisters and Mount Longdon, dominate the low ground east of Mount Kent which he needed for gun positions, to enable his artillery to reach subsequent objectives.

Thompson was greatly assisted in formulating his plans by the discovery of a map in a command post on the lower slopes of Mount Kent, abandoned when the helicopter reserve had flown to Goose Green. The map showed the regimental positions, gun areas, and other installations. It bore a striking resemblance to what was already known about the Argentine dispositions, which was very gratifying, not least to the intelligence staffs who had worked so hard at every level.

The preferred axis avoided an approach along the Fitzroy–Stanley track. An unforeseen bonus of the Fitzroy incident was to reinforce the Argentine perception alluded to before, that the main assault was to come from the south–west, possibly accompanied by an amphibious assault near Stanley. By the time the Argentines descried the direction from which the attack would come, they reacted so lethargically that no reorientation of their defences took place. Unwittingly, the British media with their obsessive doom–mongering over the Fitzroy incident, persuaded the Argentines that the British had suffered such a severe reverse that any attacks were some time off, whereas they were only three days away.

By 9 June, Moore had approved the 3 Commando Brigade plan, with the modification that Tumbledown and Mount William were allocated to 5 Infantry Brigade, to be attacked 24 hours after the first phase objectives of Longdon, Two Sisters and Mount Harriet. Thompson was given 2 Para back for his attack, and 1st Battalion Welsh Guards, with two rifle companies of 40 Commando as replacements for two of theirs who had suffered such losses of men and equipment at Fitzroy as to render them non–operational.

Thompson allocated the objectives for the first phase as follows: 3 Para, Mount Longdon, and to exploit forward on to Wireless Ridge if possible; 45 Commando, Two Sisters, and to exploit on to Tumbledown (although allocated to 5 Infantry Brigade, it would be foolish not to follow–up success if time allowed); 42 Commando, Mount Harriet, and be prepared to follow up 45 Commando through Tumbledown on to Mount William. Each of the assaulting units had a battery of 105mm light guns from 29 Commando Regiment Royal Artillery, and a frigate or destroyer with 4.5 in guns, in support. The fire from guns belonging to 4th Regiment Royal Artillery could be superimposed.

The Brigade reserve consisted of 2 Para and 1st Battalion Welsh Guards. 2 Para was ordered to follow up between 45 Commando and 3 Para, ready to reinforce either, but, if not used that night, to hook around to the north of Longdon and assault Wireless Ridge from the north at a time to be given later. 1st Battalion Welsh Guards was ordered to secure 42 Commando's start line, and be prepared to reinforce their assault if necessary. In retrospect, it was a mistake to give a strange battalion the task of securing someone else's start line. The tie–up between 42 Commando and 1st Welsh Guards was not satisfactory, and the additional complications caused by liaison in darkness, delayed 42 Commando's attack with no compensating benefit.

The jump–off time (H–Hour, when leading companies cross the start line), for each Commando or battalion, was 2001 for 3 Para, 2030 for 42 Commando, and 2100 for 45 Commando. With last light at about 1600, and moonrise at 2000, these timings would allow four to five hours for the approach march in darkness, and about nine hours for fighting through the objective with the aid of moonlight. The Argentines placed great reliance on their minefields to break up the British attacks, and also failed to appreciate the British preference for night attacks, which were beyond their ability, and consequently, in their minds, impossible. This is not the first time, nor will it be the last, that the application of one's own military standards when assessing a threat has led to a misappreciation; everybody, including the British, have been guilty.

We now know, from the official Argentine report, that Mount Longdon was held by B Company 7th Infantry Regiment, reinforced by an engineer platoon in the infantry role and about eight .50in Browning heavy machine guns manned by marines. These heavy machine guns, which out–ranged any direct–fire weapons in 3 Commando Brigade, other than those in the CVRT, which could not be used on any of the three features because of the rocky, steep terrain, were deadly in good visibility over the bare moorland slopes; an addi-

tional incentive for fighting at night.

Two Sisters was held by B Company of the 6th Argentine Infantry Regiment, and a very strong reinforced C Company of the 4th Argentine Infantry Regiment. Both company positions included .50in heavy machine guns. Four 81mm medium mortars were sited in the centre of the positions.

The remainder of 4th Argentine Infantry Regiment, sited on Mount Harriet, consisted of two rifle companies, which, with the reconnaissance platoon, two sections of 120mm heavy mortars, regimental headquarters and other headquarters, cooks and bottle–washers, and the ubiquitous heavy machine guns, were equivalent to a small battalion.

There is no reason to doubt the accuracy of the Argentine report, other than to comment that, if anything, the loser may play down his strength on a particular position in order to excuse his failure. Indeed, the maps in the Argentine report frequently show the strengths of attacking British units up to double the actual size.

Lieutenant–Colonel Pike, commanding 3 Para, chose the Murrell River as the start line for his attack, giving it the nickname FREE KICK. Similarly, he gave nicknames to other key features. His original plan was to assault the summit ridge (FLY HALF) with B Company, while A Company seized the spur running north (WING FORWARD). He subsequently planned to exploit on to Wireless Ridge with A and C Companies. He had a long approach march, but all went well until a man in B Company trod on an anti–personnel mine, alerting the Argentines.

The ensuing battle lasted until first light. The Longdon feature is rather like an alley formed by two long, parallel rock ridges running west–east. B Company's axis took them down the centre of the alley, the sides of which were held by machine gunners covered by riflemen with night sights. Every yard of the alley had to be cleared. Enemy positions, by–passed in the darkness, fired into the backs of

3 Para's battle for Mount Longdon

the soldiers advancing to the next position. An attack on a machine gun drew fire on the attacker's flank from riflemen in covering positions.

Like all the other infantry battles in this war, and most others in every war, it soon devolved into platoon, section and even individual actions. The soldiers' motivation, fieldcraft, and courage were tested time and again. In an infantry battle, particularly at night, there is plenty of scope for those who wish to retire from the contest, without actually drawing attention to themselves by running away. Only an infantry soldier has to make the individual decision to get up and go forward, again and again. Others, who fight in crews, or man guns and missile systems, do not experience this. Some, in ships for example, are taken willy–nilly whereso'er the captain orders. They have their horrors, peculiar to their calling. But it is difficult to overstate the qualities required of the infantry, and express fully the admiration one has for the young soldiers and marines on those dark mountainsides.

Eventually B Company could progress no further. A steady stream of casualties eroded their fighting strength. Sergeant McKay, having taken over when his platoon commander, Lieutenant Bickerdike was wounded, was killed taking out an enemy machine gun position single–handed. He was later awarded the Victoria Cross, posthumously.

Pike withdrew A Company, who had been unable to progress on to WING FORWARD, and pushed them through B Company. With bomb and bayonet, A Company, supported by massed GPMGs and artillery, fought their way to FULL BACK, and the long, narrow slope leading to Wireless Ridge. The position was taken. The Argentine map with their report shows Longdon being assaulted by about two battalions.

As the morning mist lifted, the enemy artillery bombarded Mount Longdon with increasing accuracy.

To the south of Mount Longdon, Whitehead, commanding 45 Commando, had opted for a two–phase attack on Two Sisters. In phase one, X Company would attack the western peak (LONG TOENAIL), which he hoped would divert the enemy's attention from Y and Z Companies' assault from the area of the Murrell Bridge on to the eastern peak (SUMMER DAYS).

Unfortunately X Company was badly delayed by the rough going, and heavy loads carried by the men. The Company was augmented by 40 Commando's Milan platoon, and, besides their own kit and ammunition, were weighed down with Milan firing posts and missiles, each forty pounds. At one point, a marine fell down a thirty–foot cliff in the darkness, but the Company second–in–command managed to resuscitate him. Instead of taking three hours for their march, X Company took six. Whitehead calmly coped as his plan unravelled, and decided to put in his phase two attack simultaneously with X Company's assault.

X Company fought its way along the western summit, as Y and Z Companies silently advanced up the bare, 250 metre high slope. About 500 metres short of the summit, they were spotted by a sentry, and were engaged by .50in heavy machine guns. Both companies were pinned down. Lieutenant Dytor, the leading troop commander of Z Company, stood up and ran forward shouting the company battle cry, 'Zulu, Zulu'; his troop followed. This broke the stalemate, as his company commander called for mortar and artillery fire from the Forward Observation Officer and Mortar Fire Controller alongside him. The whole company skirmished forward screaming 'Zulu, Zulu', firing GPMGs, 84mm and 66mm anti–tank rockets.

The enemy .50in heavy machine guns were well protected, because as the mortar and artillery fire lifted, they opened up again. Enemy mortar and artillery fire fell on both companies, wounding two of the three troop commanders in Y Company among others. Y Company joined in the fight, blasting at least one heavy machine gun position, while Z Company swept on to the crest. Two and a half hours after crossing the start line, Z Company secured its objective. Y Company passed through, but the enemy's resistance had broken, and only isolated positions gave any trouble, to be swiftly silenced. As 45 Commando reorganized on both summits, the Argentine 155mm guns opened up on the position. The Argentine map shows 45 Commando's assault by two companies on the eastern peak as a full battalion attack.

By the time 45 Commando was firmly established, it was too late to allow them to advance to Tumbledown. Thompson stopped them, although Whitehead said he was ready to go.

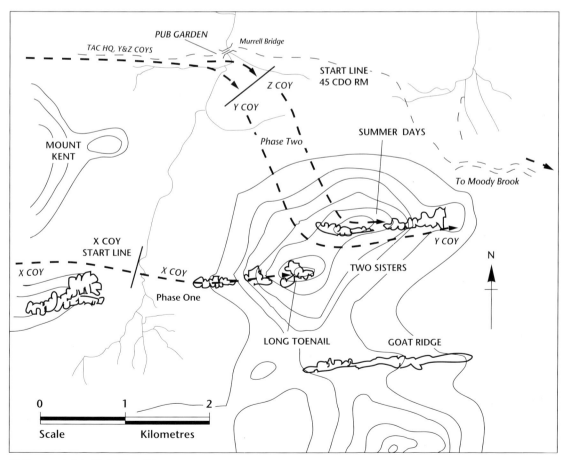

45 Commando's battle for Two Sisters

Lieutenant–Colonel Vaux, commanding 42 Commando, was faced with either a head–on assault against the strongest position on Mount Harriet, or a wide right–flanking move. If he attempted to out–flank to the north, he risked clashing with 45 Commando. Furthermore, the approaches on the north–east side of Mount Harriet are the steepest, in some places consisting of cliffs from 50 to 100 feet high.

Some excellent patrolling by junior officers and sergeants had found a route through and round the minefields guarding the western and southern approaches to Mount Harriet to a start line south–east of the position. Most of the minefields were ill–defined, and frequently unmarked. On two successive nights, patrols suffered casualties from mines: on each occasion, a marine lost a foot.

Vaux's plan was to feign an attack on the western end of Harriet, using J Company, while K and L Companies marched round to a forming–up place (FUP) to the south–east of Mount Harriet, where a convenient fence line provided a start line. Vaux had a further refinement: as the enemy machine guns disclosed their positions by firing at the J Company dummy attack, mortars would fire illuminating rounds, enabling the Milan anti–tank missile aimers sited on the eastern slopes of Wall Mountain to engage. (In 1982, the Milan was not equipped with a thermal imaging night sight.) Whereas the other two attacks that night approached silently, without preliminary bombardment, Vaux was allowed to use his artillery before the assault, to distract the enemy's attention from the move of K and L Companies, and to lend credibility to J Company's deception.

The long flanking approach march went without incident, although both Companies felt very naked against the distinctive bright yellow Falklands grass which, even without a moon, allows good visibility. However, the peat hags and cuttings provided some cover. The ground underfoot was more than usually wet, with numerous small streams, and large peaty puddles.

K Company crossed the start line first, covering nearly 700 metres, and penetrating right into the enemy rear, before opening fire. As the Company fought through these positions, L Company moved off to their left, heading for the western end of Mount Harriet. In some places, the Argentines were numbed into inaction by this attack coming in from an unexpected direction, and through the least–well defended part of the position. Their attempts to counter–attack, using troops from the western end, were frustrated by mortar and shell fire raining down on this end of the feature.

Both K and L Companies fought skilfully, well controlled by their officers and NCOs. All radios within each company were on the same frequency, and every man worked like the member of a well–drilled football team, as they fought forward to the crash of the 66mm and 84mm anti–tank rockets, blasting bunkers and sangars, and the crump and flame of their own artillery fire and mortars, and that of the enemy. During K Company's battle, Corporal Newland moved forward and single–handedly assaulted an Argentine position consisting of a GPMG and ten riflemen, eliminating the position, but was wounded himself in the process.

As with all other attacks by 3 Commando Brigade, the gunners played a major part in success. At one stage, the forward observer with K Company Commander was controlling fire from his own battery, the Commando's mortars, and a destroyer.

Just before first light, Mount Harriet was secure, and L Company was ordered to press on to Goat Ridge. They found the ridge unoccupied, but seeing about a platoon of enemy running towards Mount Tumbledown, engaged them with artillery. These were the only Argentines from the Harriet position to escape. The Argentines assessed that Mount Harriet had been attacked by about a battalion from the west, and two companies from the east.

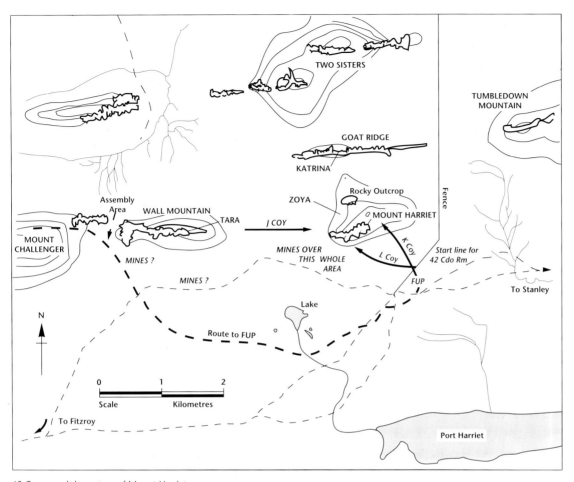

42 Commando's capture of Mount Harriet

As on the other objectives, dawn, and the bright frosty weather as the mist lifted, also brought with it increasing Argentine artillery fire. At 3 Commando Brigade Headquarters it was snowing.

It was now 5 Infantry Brigade's turn; their objectives Mount Tumbledown and Mount William, planned for the night 12/13 June. 3 Commando Brigade was not to be idle, for Wireless Ridge had yet to be taken: 2 Para's task. It was important that an attack on Wireless Ridge was mounted in concert with 5 Infantry Brigade's assault on Mount Tumbledown which overlooked the former. Therefore when Wilson properly asked for a 24–hour delay to allow more time for reconnaissance by his assaulting battalions, who had not had the benefit of 3 Commando Brigade's comprehensive patrolling to familiarize themselves with the ground, Thompson postponed the attack on Wireless Ridge. More important, the artil-lery in both brigades, beginning the previous night's battle with 480 to 500 rounds per gun, was reduced to a few rounds. There was such a short-age of helicopters, it would take at least another day to re–stock, even to 300 rounds per gun.

Wilson's original intention had been to assault from south of Mount Harriet in a north–easterly direction, north of the Fitzroy–Stanley track. He was persuaded to change his axis to an approach from Goat Ridge on to Tumble-down, followed by swinging right on to Mount William. Had he persisted with his first plan, he would have been fulfilling the enemy expec-tations exactly, and casualties would have been far higher.

Mounts Tumbledown and William were treated as one defensive position by the Argentines, being part of the 5th Argentine Marines' tactical area of responsibility, which included Sapper Hill. The Marine under-strength O Company was sited astride the

Fitzroy–Stanley track; N Company, consisting of four platoons, held the crestline and southern side of Tumbledown, with a platoon on Mount William. The layout of this company ensured that any advance up the re–entrant between Tumbledown and William would end up in a sack, the end and sides of which were held by the enemy. The western end of Tumbledown was occupied by B Company 6th Infantry Regiment, and the Marine Engineers, fighting as infantry. In addition there were the remnants of 4th, 6th, and 12th Regiments who had escaped from Mount Harriet and Two Sisters. Sapper Hill was held by M Company of the Marines.

On Tumbledown, the 5th Marines had prepared probably the strongest and best–sited position encountered in the war. Trenches and bunkers were constructed to make best use of crevices in the rocks, with natural rock formations as overhead protection wherever possible. Positions were sited to provide mutual support to each other and often to take attackers in defilade: from the side. The marine privates and junior NCOs, although conscripts, were better trained than their army counterparts. Unlike some infantry regiments, this battalion had not been split up, they had their own battery of 105mm pack howitzers, and better cold–weather clothing than the Army.

Lieutenant–Colonel Scott, commanding 2nd Battalion Scots Guards, having examined the ground from 42 Commando's positions on Goat Ridge, decided that the best way to attack Mount Tumbledown was end–on, passing his three rifle companies through each other in three phases. He preceded his main attack with a diversion about 30 minutes before. The diversionary force consisted of the Reconnaissance Platoon, headquarters clerks and drivers, a section of engineers from 9 Parachute Squadron, and a troop of CVRT, all commanded by Major Bethell. Bethell's task was to attack the marine company astride the Fitzroy–Stanley track, in the hope that the defenders of Tumbledown and Mount William would think this was the main assault.

After a brief fire–fight, which revealed that the Argentine position was stronger than he bargained for, Bethell, his task accomplished, withdrew his force. On their way back, under shell and mortar fire, they struck a minefield, and two men each lost a foot. In total they had suffered two dead and seven wounded, including Bethell. The troop leader's CVRT was destroyed by an anti–tank mine. The crew were lucky to survive. The commander of O Company was under the impression that the attack was the preliminary to the main British advance to Stanley, but no reserves were redeployed.

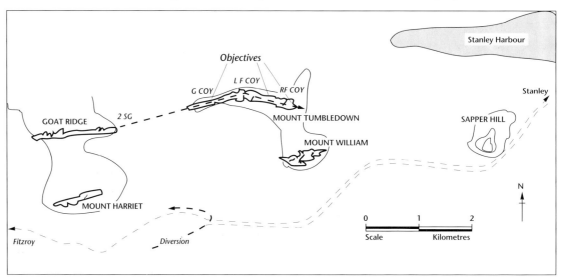

The fight for Mount Tumbledown

The first phase of the attack on Tumbledown went well, as Major Dalzel–Job's G Company moved silently forward and secured one third of the feature without opposition. At first, the second phase attack, by Major Kiszely's Left Flank Company went smoothly. But after about 30 minutes, the two leading platoons were pinned down by heavy fire, and despite every effort could make no progress. Unfortunately, at this moment, the artillery forward observer with the Company became detached from Kiszely in the dark, and although the battery commander with Scott tried to adjust fire on to the enemy, it was not effective.

A three–hour delay ensued while the gunners coped with a number of problems, including identifying a rogue gun which was firing wild. Eventually all was ready. The time was put to good use by 13 Platoon who managed to climb into a position overlooking the Argentine bunkers. With Major Kiszely leading, 14 and 15 Platoons attacked, supported from the flank by devastating fire from 13 Platoon's SLRs, 66mm and 84mm rockets, and GPMGs. The Guardsmen fought their way along 800 metres of ground without a pause, Major Kiszely bayonetting two enemy as he led the attack. As he and six men of the leading platoon and Company Headquarters reached the end of the Company objective, a burst of enemy fire from the far end of Tumbledown wounded three of them. Soon the rest of the Company came up and reorganized on the objective.

Major Price's Right Flank Company passed through Left Flank and, pushing 1 Platoon out on his left to provide fire support, he led off with 3 Platoon. The artillery was having problems again, and the only fire support available was from within the Company. As they fought through a succession of Argentine positions, Sergeant Jackson single–handedly attacked and destroyed an enemy position with grenades. Eleven and a quarter hours after crossing their start line, 2nd Battalion Scots Guards had secured Mount Tumble-

down. The Argentines assessed that the attack on Tumbledown and the diversion was the work of two battalions.

It had been a tough night for the Battalion, but they had coped magnificently. For many crucial hours they were without artillery support, and never had the advantage of the intimate and responsive fire that the Commandos and parachute battalions usually received from their gunners. Close affiliations and exercises for over 20 years had led to a mutual trust and expertise between gunners and infantry in 3 Commando Brigade. Regimental spirit and discipline sustained the Scots Guards in a battle that would have daunted most other infantry battalions taken straight from public duties, with so little time to prepare.

The postponement of the attack on Wireless Ridge allowed Lieutenant–Colonel Chaundler, now in command of 2 Para, the opportunity to examine the ground from 3 Para's position on Mount Longdon, and brief his company commanders. Following the Battalion's experience at Goose Green, when they were critically short of fire support, Chaundler asked for, and was given the maximum fire support available. He had two batteries of 105mm light guns, one and subsequently two, frigates (a frigate with an automatic 4.5in gun can lay down the equivalent fire to a battery of six 105mm guns), the mortars of 3 Para in addition to his own, and a troop of CVRT.

The ground over which 2 Para was to attack consisted of parallel, open, rolling, boggy ridges, much less steep and lower than the other objectives around Stanley attacked so far. Except on Wireless Ridge itself, there were no rocky spinebacks; and even this was a miniature of those on the other mountain positions. Chaundler's plan was a framework, designed for maximum flexibility and capable of amendment at short notice. The Battalion was a worked–up team, with the experience of the Goose Green battle on which to draw. Chaundler planned a four–phase noisy attack

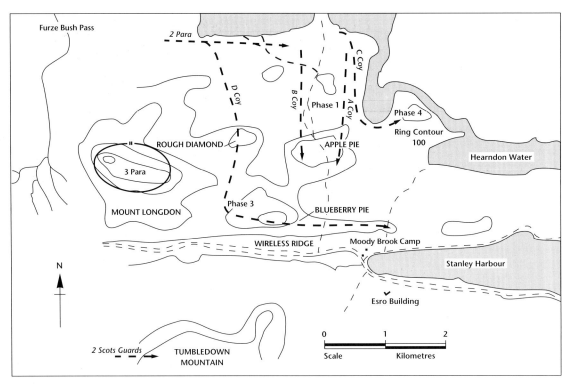

2 Para's fight for Wireless Ridge

(with preliminary bombardment). In phase one, D Company would capture the feature north-east of Longdon (ROUGH DIAMOND). In phase two, A and B Companies would attack ring contour 250 (APPLE PIE). In phase three, D Company would attack Wireless Ridge (BLUEBERRY PIE), from the west, supported by fire from A and B Companies. In phase four, C Company would attack ring contour 100.

The registration of the fire plan was interrupted by four enemy Skyhawks bombing 3 Commando Brigade Headquarters, one of the batteries supporting 2 Para, and attacking the helicopters *en route* to lift the Battalion's machine gun and mortar platoons forward. Last–minute adjustments to the mortar and artillery targets were made after dark using illuminating rounds. In the forming up position, just after last light, Chaundler was told that there was a minefield in front of APPLE PIE and that Wireless Ridge was held by two companies, not one. He decided to press on. It started to snow.

2 Para's objective was held by 7th Argentine Infantry Regiment. We now know that C Company held ROUGH DIAMOND, A Com-

pany held APPLE PIE, and that Wireless Ridge was held by a reinforced company and the Regimental Headquarters. One company of the 3rd Argentine Infantry Regiment occupied a position just south of Wireless Ridge, astride the track about a kilometre west of Moody Brook Camp.

At 2145 D Company crossed the start line. They found that the enemy on ROUGH DIAMOND had withdrawn, leaving a few dead behind. As the Company reorganized they were hit by enemy 155mm air–burst. Major Neame ordered them forward, out of the enemy defensive fire task. A and B Companies also found APPLE PIE deserted. The storm of fire had totally demoralized the enemy. The main problem was the speed with which the Argentines shelled their own recently–vacated positions. Chaundler decided to bring forward C Company's attack on ring contour 100. This too was found to be deserted. As D Company marched to its start line at the west of Wireless Ridge, the CVRT, Milans, and machine gunners moved up to join A and B Companies on APPLE PIE.

D Company cleared the first part of the objective without any trouble, but encountered stiff resistance on the second part. During the fight for this position, the forward observer with D Company called down fire on his own position by mistake, killing one soldier and wounding some others. An easily made error in snow flurries in the dark. Suddenly the enemy broke and ran, chivvied off the ridge by fire from the CVRT with their excellent night sights, and pursued by D Company. A half–hearted Argentine counter–attack was easily repulsed.

The Battalion had fought a model all–arms battle. The troop of CVRT had played a major part in achieving victory at such low cost. The Argentines believed that the whole Wireless Ridge position had been attacked by a battalion and two companies from the north, and two companies from Mount Longdon.

Soon after first light on 14 June, the Gurkhas were preparing for an assault on Mount William. On their move up they had come under artillery fire and lost two men wounded. The Battalion arrived on Mount William to find the Argentines had gone. The Argentine Army was streaming back into Stanley.

It was almost over. There was a brisk fire–fight, when a troop of A Company 40 Commando under command of the Welsh Guards, was landed by mistake by helicopter on Sapper Hill, instead of south–west of Mount William, after the cease–fire had been ordered. The Argentine artillery continued firing almost up to the moment of cease–fire, despite the rest of their army being in full retreat.

The attack by 3 Commando Brigade,

Jubilant Islanders hold Major–General Jeremy Moore aloft in the early hours of 15 June after the official surrender of Argentine forces. *Press Association*

ordered for the night 14/15 June, would not be necessary. The Commando Brigade was led into Stanley by 2 Para, closely followed by 3 Para and 42 Commando. Sapper Hill was secured by 45 Commando and the Welsh Guards. While the Scots Guards spent a second freezing night on Tumbledown, surrounded by the debris of battle.

The land campaign was over. The laurels for the British success on land must go to the junior officers, non–commissioned officers, soldiers and marines, irrespective of their task, whatever their cap badge. They endured, doing all that was asked and more, sustained by training, regimental spirit, and matchless humour.

The Army's Infantry and Armoured Reconnaissance Forces

Brigadier Hew Pike (Commanding Officer, 3rd Battalion The Parachute Regiment, Falklands War)

It has been said that if the Battle of Waterloo was won on the playing fields of Eton, then the Falklands War was won on the training fields of Brecon and Dartmoor. There is threefold truth in this statement, for it hints not only at the arduous character of the training at both these places, but also at the part they play in developing, for the infantry and the Royal Marines, non–commissioned officers whose calibre is, in my experience, unrivalled by any other nation. Most significantly of all, perhaps, the statement rightly implies that the action on land during the Falklands Campaign was pre–eminently an 'Infantryman's War', in a way that, for example, the Sinai Campaign of 1967 or the Gulf War of 1991 were not. This is not to suggest that the infantry could have done it alone. For a start they were greatly assisted by a mistakenly small force, totalling in firepower terms only four Scorpions and four Scimitars, from the Blues and Royals, of whom more later. Even more importantly, without the Royal Artillery, Royal Engineers, Royal Signals, Army Air Corps and logistic support, which together generate the fighting power of the combined arms battle, then the infantry would have foundered. Naval gunfire and close air support by Harrier GR3 also played crucial parts in the land campaign. The fact remains that this was a war to recapture territory, which, from the capture of the San Carlos bridgehead through to the capture of Port Stanley, could only be done by the infantry. This was a marching war, a war of night attacks to capture key objectives, a war of close–quarter fighting, a war of patrol-

ling, a war over arduous terrain in generally foul weather. A war, in short, in the winning of which the skills and resources of the infantry-man were critical.

In this sense a professional army clearly had a huge advantage over one made up pre-dominantly of peasant conscripts. The British battalions were much better trained than their opponents, and knew it. Furthermore, the de-termination to prove professional skills, when such chances come so rarely, is a force in adversity at least as powerful as patriotism or regimental spirit. Add to this the close com-radeship which tough and demanding training breeds in men, and the keen rivalry between marine, parachute and Guards battalions, and the result is a formidable collective will to win.

Yet, for all this, hindsight can beguile. From the sailing of the Task Force to the final surrender, there were a multitude of deadly risks and uncertainties, and in such an atmos-phere there was little evidence of over–confi-dence–only an iron determination to see the thing through to the finish, and the quicker the better. Because of these many uncertainties – the greatest one always being, 'How will the enemy fight?', I believe that the battle of Dar-win/Goose Green was a tangible and very real turning–point in the land war. This is not because it was a key objective – many would argue that it could have been blanked off and ignored – nor because of the high numbers who surrendered there. It is because before Goose Green, we understood that we had to win, whilst after it, we knew that we would. In other words, it was the moral turning–point, the kick–start that was needed after the difficult early days in the San Carlos bridgehead, with air attacks seriously dislocating the logistic build–up of the landing force. It was this battle, fought by 2 Para, with almost no all–arms support, which captured the prize of moral supremacy from our enemy, after which, despite the importance of subsequent battles, it became a question not of whether, but when, as Clausewitz has it, 'his courage would be killed'.

The Army's infantry and armoured contribution to the landing force was, of course, all concentrated in 3 Commando Brigade until the subsequent arrival in theatre of 5 Infantry Brigade. In this chapter we are concerned only with the performance of army units, and, while looking at these, we therefore need constantly to bear in mind the all–arms make–up of 3 Commando Brigade, comprising five battalions (40, 42 and 45 Commando, 2 and 3 Para), two armoured reconnaissance troops of the Blues and Royals, and its full range of supporting arms and services.

3 Para remained with 3 Commando Brigade throughout the campaign, whilst 2 Para was transferred to 5 Brigade during the early days of June, returning to the Marines for the crucial mountain battles leading to the surrender. The 2nd Scots Guards, 1st Welsh Guards and 1/7th Gurkhas formed the three battalions of 5 Brigade. The Blues and Royals operated initially with 3 Commando Brigade and subsequently were allocated by the Divisional Commander, General Moore, where they were felt to be most needed. But it was the commander of 3 Commando Brigade, Brigadier Thompson, who was declared by General Moore to be 'the man of the match' after the surrender, and this reflects not only his personal performance as a commander but the central role played by his brigade and all its units, from landing to surrender. In 5 Brigade, only the Scots Guards were called upon to fight a major battle, for Mount Tumbledown.

The organization of the five army battalions was broadly similar, although both parachute battalions had a patrol company, whose four–man reconnaissance skills proved particularly important during the long advances and before night attacks. All battalions had 81mm mortar and Milan anti–tank platoons, the carriage of whose weapons and ammunition proved a major test of improvisation and toughness. The General Purpose Machine Gun (GPMG), with which all sections were equipped, was also used in the more specialized, sustained–fire role; this again demanded the manpacking of tripods, dial sights and large quantities of ammunition. In the three rifle companies of each battalion, platoons were equipped with HE and phosphorus grenades, 66mm light anti–tank weapons (M72), (nor-

A Rifleman of 1/7th Gurkha Rifles mans a General Purpose Machine Gun aboard *Queen Elizabeth II*. The gun is mounted for anti–aircraft defence.
7th Duke of Edinburgh's Own Gurkha Rifles

mally 12 per platoon, this weapon proved particularly effective against bunker and trench positions), one 84mm medium anti–tank weapon (Carl Gustav) and the 2in light mortar for local illumination. Stretcher–bearers formed from the drivers, cooks and mechanics of each battalion's echelon, most of whom were not needed in their primary role, carried forward ammunition supplies as normal procedure.

During the weeks at sea, much thought and training had gone on to achieve the most punch for the least weight. This was one of the many areas where a weighty reality of war had tended to be skimped in peacetime training – blank ammunitions and a few pyrotechnics stuffed into smock pockets did not pose the same problems of personal organization or endurance. In many other respects, the voyage south had given time to 'bone up on the basics' – fire team drills, weapon skills, battlefield first aid, navigation, and a host of other battle-winning techniques that tended to be neglected amongst all the distractions of peacetime barrack life. Physical fitness was also, of course, a high priority – and was to prove its worth not only in the long marches, but in the resilience

Heavily–laden Scots Guardsmen of 5 Infantry Brigade come ashore at San Carlos, 2 June.
Airborne Forces Museum

of those badly wounded in overcoming their injuries. So far as the general state of training of the battalions is concerned, there were certainly differences at the outset. Of the two

parachute battalions, one was the Army's 'Spearhead Battalion', the other about to start a six–month tour in Belize. There was also, in these battalions, an innate self–confidence and an offensive spirit which their demanding process of selection and training generated. The Gurkha battalion was also in good shape, as part of 5 Infantry Brigade's peacetime order of battle. The two Guards battalions, conversely, inevitably felt the effects of their public duties role during their work–up training at Sennybridge. The Blues and Royals were also well–organized and prepared, from their training on board the *Canberra* and having had the chance to live–fire and calibrate their equipment on Ascension Island. All the battalions of 3 Commando Brigade had been thoroughly drilled in the procedures and techniques for amphibious assault landing whilst at Ascension.

Despite the generally high standard of training, the campaign was to prove again the words of Clausewitz that 'the soldier, high or low, should not have to encounter in war, things which, seen for the first time, set him in terror or perplexity'. Familiarity breeds confidence, and is reassuring in battle. Young soldiers, some not even 18 years old, not surprisingly needed strong leadership from their officers and NCOs. In particular, they took time to adjust mentally to the 'open–ended' nature of their commitment, compared with the training exercise of known duration. They quickly realized that they really must look after themselves with supreme competence and organization in the field, if they were to survive. Similarly, the war demonstrated how important it was for the leaders in a battalion to possess the robustness and resilience to rise above hardship and misfortune, and still command. Some found the conditions so demanding that they had little or no energy left to think clearly, let alone lead others. In adversity men looked to those leaders able to take it in their stride.

Another significant weakness, not only in battalions, but throughout both brigades, lay in combined arms integration. My own battalion, for example, did not have an affiliated artillery battery – my Battery Commander and Forward Observation Officers only joined us at Ascension. There was little understanding of the capabilities of the Scorpions and Scimitars, which were not used at Goose Green and really only exploited their potential in one battle – the assault across Wireless Ridge. Notwithstanding the serious logistic constraints of the early days, and the difficulties caused by weather and terrain in moving guns and ammunition between positions, it is no coincidence that the Commando Brigade fought its first battle – Goose Green – with minimal all–arms support to the battalion, and its last battle – Wireless Ridge – with all available firepower pounding the enemy.

At every level, the orchestration of the combined arms battle in order to maximize success and minimize casualties improved steadily as the campaign unfolded.

In defence, traditionally the British Army's strongest suit, the battalions with their armoured recce support put up staunch performances, although never seriously threatened by enemy ground attack. In the San Carlos bridgehead, the main concern was protection from air attack and the possibility of action against the landing force by the Argentine so–called 'Strategic Reserve', helicopter–borne, and based, it was thought, at Darwin. Our deployments were therefore planned with this in mind, as well as the danger of enemy patrols infiltrating to disrupt the build–up of logistic stocks and installations. The Blues and Royals CVRs were deployed for surveillance by night – exploiting their Image Intensifications, X10 sights – and for the destruction of helicopters as they landed, by day. The Milan anti–tank teams and GPMG (SF) were also deployed against the helicopter threat. The infantrymen dug themselves into the rocks, and quickly developed the skills of improvisation needed to be both effective and comfortable. The 81mm mortar base plates, for

example, either sank into soft peat or slid out of position over rock just below the ground crust. Local hard core, and other farm materials, were needed to overcome the problem of soft ground. Difficulty with hard ground was less readily resolved and, during the offensive phase of the campaign, there were four broken ankles in one mortar platoon alone, as crews desperately fought to keep their base plates steady during firing in support of attacks. Meanwhile, many positions quickly hit the water table, and needed either to move or build up, with rocks and peat, if life was to be reasonably safe and bearable. After the excitement and sense of achievement that came from splashing ashore and liberating the settlement of San Carlos and Port San Carlos, the battalions settled down into a routine of getting comfortable and secure and awaiting further orders. Air attacks were principally directed against shipping, and caused little concern on land, once the initial alarm of over–flying enemy aircraft had been overcome, and the occasional shrapnel scatterings from parachute–retarded bombs accepted. The slow–flying Pucara ground attack aircraft were a nastier prospect, and carried out intermittent sorties against British positions throughout the war. The Blowpipe missile detachments with each battalion were sometimes able to engage these aircraft as they attacked, and a number were accounted for by Blowpipe missiles or by small–arms fire. The Pucara was also a particular threat to helicopters. At this stage, no enemy artillery was able to join the debate – the experience of this particularly dangerous and potentially psychologically devastating aspect of defensive operations was to await the capture of objectives round Port Stanley.

Defence of the bridgehead did involve intensive patrolling, especially as at this stage no one knew 'what was really out there'. Intelligence provided by Special Forces during the Advance Force Operations before the landings had been of priceless value, not least in con-

A Browning .50in machine gun provides anti-aircraft cover as 5 Infantry Brigade comes ashore at San Carlos, 2 June. *Soldier: Magazine of the British Army*

firming that San Carlos remained clear of significant enemy forces. But now there was a general lack of information on detailed dispositions as they affected particular battalion operations. SAS/SBS forces were being employed in other ways. The patrolling skills of the battalions therefore became increasingly important, particularly during the advance across East Falkland and before battalion attacks. Some patrol—

at night. Extensive use was made of image intensification equipment, some of which was still 'first generation' and therefore extremely heavy and cumbersome. Some lighter equipment (for example, the Pocketscope) was also available, but there was considerable envy when we captured Argentine positions and discovered American equipment significantly superior to our own. General Slim had observed in the 14th Army that patrol skills provided a measure of just how good each battalion was, and they certainly played an important part in the battle for domination and moral supremacy. As an example of the lack of real–time intelligence, the only air photograph available of Mount Longdon before its capture by 3 Para was one taken from 10,000 feet some years before!

As we launched ourselves on the long forward advance, we were more than ever grateful for the excellent windproof smocks and trousers with which all battalions had been issued, in place of the smocks and lightweight trousers we used in Europe. The quilted suits, with zip–on trousers, were also literally life–savers, as they enabled us to leave sleeping bags and bergens as 'follow–up' equipment; they were carried rolled up in each soldier's belt–order, and used for halts when there was time for sleep to be at least attempted, aided by the excellent karrimats which everyone had with them. Many soldiers had their own boots, and were glad of them, for the issue boot at that time did not give good protection against wet and frost even when daubed with silicone wax, Mars oil and every other imaginable patent preparation. Some soldiers in more static roles used NBC overboots most successfully. Helmets were always carried and worn in contact; out of contact the inelegant arctic hat, keeping heads deliciously warm, became a lot more popular than the beret.

The two brigades closed on the high ground around Port Stanley in very different ways. In 3 Commando Brigade, two battalions – 3 Para and 45 Commando – achieved the distinction of marching all the way, capturing and liberating Douglas Settlement, Teal Inlet and Estancia as they advanced. In 5 Brigade, movement involved LSLs, assault craft and helicopters as well as the boot. But however it was done, self–sufficiency and keeping the tenuous logistic link working were the key considerations. Some vital battle–winners, such as mortar bombs, Milan and Blowpipe missiles, just could not be manpacked in large numbers. Already in the bridgehead, battalions had learnt to use local farm transport, and the gallant goodwill of the locals, to ferry supplies up to company positions in the rocks. Now, in addition to the few Volvo Bandwagons (BVs) supporting each battalion, tractors and trailers, crawler tractors towing sledges, as well as the occasional Chinook sortie, were all essential work–horses in keeping battalions linked with what they needed to fight. Particularly so, since, as we advanced, we had little idea about

when and how we might have to do so. No one knew for sure, for example, what enemy forces or minefields lay in our path around Teal Inlet or Estancia. More tractors and Falkland Islanders joined us from outlying settlements like Green Patch as we moved eastwards. In 3 Para, two Islanders, Terry Peck and Vernon Steen, had linked up in Port San Carlos, having escaped from Port Stanley soon after the invasion of early April. They acted as invaluable and very courageous guides throughout the campaign.

Every man also carried his essential fighting and survival equipment as he stumbled by night over rocks, tussocks, stream and bog towards the next objective. The dehydrated arctic rations, cooked on hexamine burners, were well worth carrying – light and versatile. A combination of oatmeal, apple flakes and powdered milk made an excellent breakfast of hot porridge. Ammunition was carried in the pouches attached to belt–order and in bergens. First–aid supplies and the battalion's full range of man pack radios with spare batteries also had to be carried in every platoon.

A Chinook helicopter delivers supplies and equipment to 3 Para at Teal Inlet. *Airborne Forces Museum*

Yet, for all its challenges and uncertainties, the advance towards Port Stanley had a strangely familiar feel to it. We had done this kind of thing so often on exercises, and even the terrain was so like Dartmoor or Sennybridge, that it was our opponents from the hills of Argentina for whom we sometimes felt sorry, rather than ourselves. Many men in the marine Commandos and parachute battalions had the feeling that the Almighty had arranged this particular war especially for them. Above all, the advance east meant that we were getting somewhere, closing with our enemy, and thus nearer finishing the whole business quickly and successfully. This was the time when every patrol and section commander became like a father–figure to his young charges, encouraging, cajoling, checking, explaining – even though he knew little more than they, most of the time, about future intentions.

One particularly significant feature of these marches was the performance of the CVR(T) of the Blues and Royals. Commanders were cautious about ordering them forward over such unpredictable terrain, but their troop leaders and crews had no such doubts. Determined to prove their value, they negotiated the rolling, windswept hills and valleys with great skill, and although night movement proved generally inadvisable, by day they rapidly closed with their infantry comrades, eager to support them in whatever tasks lay ahead.

The battles to capture key objectives, all but Goose Green fought at night, were the very essence of the infantry's contribution to victory, and the ultimate test of each attacking battalion's courage and fighting power. The story of each battle is well known. What is perhaps most interesting are the unchanging lessons of such battles, all of which would have been familiar to our fathers and grandfathers. Yet no one, in either brigade, from brigadier downwards, had any experience of such actions, and no amount of history is a substitute for experience. Above all, I believe, the Falklands impressed upon us all just how long such battles can take, and hence how important is the sustained rate of all forms of direct and indirect fire to success, in breaking the enemy's will.

The orchestration of firepower, the 'great persuader', improved steadily as the campaign progressed. At Goose Green, 2 Para were very much on their own, with inadequate support from their own mortars, let alone guns. A Harrier GR3 sortie came at a particularly critical and opportune moment, but the Battalion emerged from their famous victory, vowing that next time it would all be very different. On Wireless Ridge, it certainly was. For not only did they have the Scorpions and Scimitars of the Blues and Royals providing devastating direct fire to supplement their own, on relatively open ground where the CVRs could cover each other from position to position, but they also had a number of batteries with fireplans closely linked to the progress of the ground battle. The mortar platoons of both parachute battalions added their contribution, and this battle certainly represents the high point of all–arms integration in this particular campaign. The old adage of Rommel's, to 'plaster the enemy with fire', was well vindicated, in reducing casualties and in breaking the enemy's will.

If this 'plastering' could be linked with a flanking manoeuvre, as for example on Mount Harriet – 42 Commando's objective – then the chances of swift victory at minimum cost were greatly enhanced. Such flanking movements were not always possible – for example on Mount Longdon or Mount Tumbledown – when terrain or enemy positions in depth prohibited the option. Even then, it was essential to try to achieve surprise, and here the Argentines played into our hands. They seemed unaware of the philosophy of 'aggressive defence', whereby surveillance, a reconnaissance screen, ambushes, observation linked to Indirect Fire Tasks, and raiding forces are used to disrupt the ordered build–up of an attacking force. Battalions were therefore able to close with their objectives without interference, using the night and stealth as cover. All that interfered with them were the ubiquitous minefields which the enemy had laid, some of which were known from patrolling, others not. They were not generally very deep, linked with wire, or covered by fire, and therefore the tactic was simply to press on. Despite the serious injuries sustained by some soldiers on mines, this was the right approach.

Plastering and outflanking notwithstanding, the 'break–in' and 'fight–through' stages of each battle proved to be the greatest testing grounds of leadership. For the battalion commander, his forward presence was certainly needed, giving him the ability to intervene, commit reserves, or reallocate firepower when needed. The action of Colonel Jones at Goose Green, in restoring momentum to a stalled battle, stands out as an example both of supreme gallantry and real tactical leadership. But, generally, it was the company commander who had his objectives, and must find ways around the resistance he encountered in reaching it. Even more so was it the junior leader, at platoon, section, and fire team level, who now faced his supreme test. Here, example was everything if men were to keep moving and outmanoeuvre enemy trenches or bunkers. The fight–through often proved a long, costly process. At very close quarters with the enemy, every resource of fieldcraft and weaponry was needed to take out each position. More often crawling than running or standing, grenades (both HE and phosphorus – the latter much more effective) and the light anti–tank weapon, were used to cause at least momentary shock, and some casualties, so that each small assault group could close with the position and kill those remaining. Their movements were closely tied in with supporting fire from Milan and GPMG (SF) fire teams, whilst mortar and artillery fire was also used with increasing skill and accuracy, very close indeed to our own assaulting groups. This murderous phase of battle was made worse by the frequent attentions of enemy artillery, which tracked the progress of attacking forces with uncanny accuracy. In the mountains, fixed heavy machine gun positions and skilled snipers also repre-

sented particularly lethal threats. In one instance, on Mount Longdon, a three–man Milan crew were all killed by one 105mm recoilless rifle round, as they tried to move to a better supporting position.

The capture of Goose Green, Mount Longdon, Two Sisters, Mount Harriet, Mount Tumbledown, and Wireless Ridge, proved the will of the attackers over that of the defenders. These bloody encounters with the enemy, physically and mentally draining, demonstrated that the training and courage of the British Infantry of the 1980s was equal at least to that of earlier generations.

The system of 'casevac', first–aid and surgery to support these battles was naturally of the utmost importance to both life and morale.

3 Para sets up camp at Estancia House and rests after its long 'tab' towards Stanley. *Airborne Forces Museum*

The first requirement was a very high standard of battle first–aid, so that soldiers could help their comrades when the tactical situation allowed. Each company also had at least one medical NCO, and stretcher–bearers following up behind each engagement were organized on battalion lines. At the Regimental Aid Post, well forward with the battle too, the battalion's doctor provided further life–saving first–aid, before the soldier was moved back to the nearest Field Surgical Team. This part of the journey was by helicopter, if possible, and the Army Air Corps pilots performed extraordinary feats of skill and courage in lifting out the wounded under fire, often in appalling weather. Sometimes, if enemy artillery fire was too heavy, or night or bad weather prevented flying (there were very few pilots trained with Night Vision Goggles at this time, and little equipment), the journey had to be undertaken by Volvo BV. In the case of 3 Para, for example, the RAP was based under the western lee of Mount Longdon and the Field Surgical Team at Teal Inlet. Because the Battalion was subjected to constant artillery and mortar fire in the 48 hours between the capture of Longdon and of Tumbledown, from where the enemy OPs could observe us closely and accurately, it was frequently too hazardous for a helicopter to fly in. The casualty would therefore be taken by Volvo BV back to an intermediate point, where he could safely be picked up by helicopter. Overall, the casevac system was a triumph of ingenuity and determination, at every level – first–aiders, stretcher bearers, medical NCOs,

pilots, doctors and surgeons. Without them all, the infantry could not have done their job.

The infantry and armoured reconnaissance forces who fought in the Falklands War did so with less–than–perfect organizations, training and equipment. This will ever be the case, although a good army will always strive to achieve the highest possible standards, with the best available equipment. What really counts, however – as it always has done – is the quality of the men and their leaders, and hence their ability to find ways around difficulties, their confidence in adversity, their resourcefulness in misfortune, their determination to vindicate professional skills well learned and practised. In short, what really counts is the will to win, generated through demanding training, and in this war the infantry battalions and their Household Cavalry comrades were not found wanting.

South Atlantic Medal 1982 with rosette. Awarded to Rifleman Ombhakta Gurung, 7th Duke of Edinburgh's Own Gurkha Rifles. The obverse shows a crowned head of the Queen facing right; the reverse shows the Armorial bearings of the Crown Colony of the Falkland Islands and its Dependencies, encompassed by the legend, 'South Atlantic Medal' and sprigs of laurel.
National Army Museum 9102-1

The Gunners

Major-General Brian Pennicott (Commander, Royal Artillery, Falklands War)

I should begin by explaining the part I played in the Falklands War. In early May, about a month after the naval Task Force, which included a reinforced 3 Commando Brigade, had sailed, I was appointed to Major–General Moore's Headquarters as, initially, his artillery adviser and later, on our arrival in the Falklands, as his overall artillery commander.

On joining General Moore's Headquarters at Northwood it soon became very clear that there would be inadequate artillery to support a two–brigade division properly. Ideally one should have Close Support Batteries on the scale of one for each Royal Marine Commando or infantry battalion, General Support guns in sufficient numbers adequately to fight the battle in depth, sufficient air defence assets such that none of the ground troops need to fight outside air defence cover and, finally, locating assets sufficient to acquire targets in depth as well as intelligence. Despite the efforts of Major–General Moore and his staff we were to be short of much of this. Our claims for more artillery were rejected on the grounds of insufficient shipping space and, I sense, a firm conviction that the reinforced 3 Commando Brigade would be sufficient to win the land campaign and that 5 Infantry Brigade were really being sent as garrison troops only. How wrong our masters were proved to be, and nothing highlighted this more than the loss of so many lives on *Sir Galahad* when it was attacked by enemy aircraft. Our total medium–level air defence assets throughout the early

stages of the campaign were 12 Rapiers. These were deployed initially to cover San Carlos with its shipping, hospital, major supplies and command facilities. Once 3 Commando Brigade had gone firm in the area of Teal, four Rapiers were sent to give air defence cover leaving the bare minimum of eight to safeguard San Carlos. It was not until the RAF Regiment Rapiers arrived and could be moved into San Carlos that we were in a position to deploy some to Fitzroy. Unfortunately the earliest that they could move was with the *Sir Galahad*.

As an artillery commander in amphibious operations I was not only responsible for advising the overall commander and for commanding the Gunner assets available but also for running the Supporting Arms Co–ordination Centre (SACC). The SACC is the means by which the air space over the area of the land battle is managed such that there is no conflict of friendly forces. It consists of officers covering Close Support Artillery, Air Defence Artillery, Naval Gunfire Support, Light and Support helicopters and Fixed Wing Aircraft. Initially the staff given to me to run the SACC was totally inadequate but, with a little cajoling and some hard talking, sufficient staff were made available, though never more than the bare minimum. This shortfall in manpower together with an insufficiency of the right communications was to mean that while I was able to exercise adequate control I was never capable of commanding, in particular, the Close Support Regiments. This was solved by grouping artillery assets under their respective brigades and making the Commanding Officers of the regiments responsible for providing their own fire support, their local air defence, their logistic requirements and for moving, under my orders, their batteries. This they did superbly!

The first phase of the land battle was to move ashore and secure a beach–head in the San Carlos area. This was achieved successfully but was immediately followed by an air defence battle of a severity not experienced since World War II. Our twelve Rapier equipments, which were to provide our medium–level air defence capability, were flown ashore to a deployment plan worked out on the

being deployed by helicopter when the first air attacks happened, and were quickly dropped, often on to spots which were not ideal but at which they had to remain. At least initially, the Rapiers gave cause for great concern. On that first day ashore up to eight of the launchers were to be unserviceable at any one time; but then no one took into account that they were old, first–generation launchers, highly sensitive and not designed for the rough passage they had suffered on board the ships or when being flown ashore. The skill and perseverance of the detachments together with a massive move of spare parts by the RAF improved this situation but throughout the campaign it was

A 105mm light gun is loaded aboard *Europic Ferry* at Southampton. The ship sailed on 19 April, carrying much of 2 Para's equipment and three Scout helicopters.
Soldier: Magazine of the British Army

computer at Royal Signals and Radar Establishment at Malvern. This proved necessary as there was no way of doing the normal reconnaissance which could ensure proper coverage of the area from the best locations. As it was, some of the Rapiers were in the process of

to be a headache. This, in turn, was to add a considerable strain on our limited and overworked support helicopter fleet.

Apart from the task of keeping their launchers serviceable, the Rapier detachments were faced with many challenges. They were unable to use their surveillance radars because of the density of our own helicopters flying within the San Carlos area, and they were presented with fast, low flying Argentine aircraft at close range and at levels quite often below their own position. They were forced to acquire, track, and fire upon enemy aircraft within the space of some five seconds – nothing like the scenarios they had been presented with in training! Despite this they managed to shoot down 13 Argentine aircraft!

Having secured the beach–head the breakout began. No one will forget the heroic deeds performed by 2 Para in their march to and then the relief of Darwin and Goose Green. This remarkable feat was achieved with insufficient artillery support. The helicopter lift available to this operation only allowed for three guns and 200 rounds of ammunition per gun to be deployed. This shortfall was compounded by the Naval Gunfire Support Ships' computer going out of action at a critical time. This lesson was well learnt, for when they went into action again in the battle for Wireless Ridge the Commanding Officer of 2 Para and ourselves ensured that sufficient firepower was available by using two batteries of artillery, two troops of light armour, and an NGS ship, as well as their own mortars and machine guns. As a result Wireless Ridge was taken relatively easily!

The success at Darwin/Goose Green was swiftly followed by the move of 3 Para and 45 Commando to Estancia and Teal respectively. Once secure, these two units, reinforced by 42 Commando, closed up to the enemy positions and began offensive patrolling and preparation for what we knew would follow. Remember, all of this was done on foot because of the atrocious conditions under which we operated. The sub–antarctic weather which could change from bright, clear but cold to storm conditions in a matter of minutes, together with an unwelcoming terrain of peat, large tussocks of strong grass and rocky outcrops made movement by foot difficult and by vehicle almost impossible. Only our light, tracked, armoured vehicles and

the limited number of Volvo over–snow vehicles managed to move reasonably easily. Naturally, as the infantry battalions and Royal Marines moved forward their Gunner support did likewise. For those who travelled on foot – the Battery Commanders, the Naval Gunfire Support Forward Observers and the Forward Observation Officers – the need to lighten loads was soon very obvious. Quickly their binoculars became monoculars, their heavy, cumbersome but very useful laser range–finders were left behind, to come forward only when firm in positions they would occupy for days rather than hours. The movement of guns themselves and their ammunition was particularly difficult. Let me explain: to move a battery of 6 x 105mm light guns, the men, one command post and two hundred rounds of ammunition per gun, was a 45 x Sea King helicopter lift. Clearly that number of Sea King helicopters was never available and so moves became rather lengthy affairs even over quite short distances. By the time it came to the final battles, and I wished to have 500 rounds per gun on the gun position and a further 500 rounds per gun in the nearby Brigade Maintenance Area, then almost the whole of the support helicopter fleet was committed to us. There was, of course, a price to pay for this and all too frequently the commandos and infantry were to go short of food and water. The movement forward of 3 Commando Brigade followed by 5 Infantry Brigade, together with the supporting arms, was to take a long time mainly because of our shortage of support helicopters.

By the time we were ready for Phase 1 of our final push to retake Port Stanley – the assaults on Two Sisters, Mount Harriet and Mount Longdon – we, the Gunners, had been in action for some days firing Harassing Fire tasks to disrupt the enemy and in support of numerous reconnaissance and fighting patrols sent out by the Royal Marines and Paras. It was at this stage that many of our other problems were to come to light. The first was the shortage of intelligence of what was happening beyond the immediate area of the contact battle. Whilst Special Forces patrols were working deep into enemy territory their input into the overall intelligence picture was, of course, fairly local. We tried to solve this problem, in part, by tasking the Harriers in the photo–reconnaissance role but with only limited success. They were frequently prevented from flying low enough to get good pictures either by the Argentine air defences or by poor weather or both. We badly missed the information a Drone could give us (a remotely piloted vehicle which follows a pre–programmed flight path and takes photographs which can be interpreted later), such that at the end of the campaign it was judged to be the one piece of equipment that above all we would liked to have had. Neither did we have any sound–ranging equipment which would have afforded us a gun–locating capability. We did, however, have the Cymbeline Mortar Locating equipment which was used with mixed success. It proved to be of particular value in tracking enemy helicopters.

Major problems were experienced on the gun positions when we began to fire at intense rates in support of final battles prior to the Argentine surrender. Perhaps the greatest of these was the reception on to and distribution around the gun positions of very large quantities of ammunition. There never seemed to be enough men to move ammunition, unpack it, and, after firing, dispose of the cartridge cases. This was only solved by reducing the gun detachments to minimum manning and using the rest together with cooks, REME fitters, pay clerks and signallers as ammunition handlers. To add to the problems the ground in most gun positions was such that during sustained firing the gun carriages sank up to the layer's seat, after firing as little as thirty rounds. On some positions the guns not only sank but would move back up to ten yards at the same time. This meant that guns were continually being taken out of action before being surveyed back into position again. During this last

The first 105mm gun to be fired in the Falklands. 79 Commando Battery engaging machine gun nests that shot down Gazelle helicopters, San Carlos, 1817 'Zulu' Time (GMT), 21 May. *Courtesy of Major P N Bates*

stage guns were firing an average of 250 rounds per gun, which illustrated the workload in terms of ammunition handling and the frustration caused by having to dig out and realign the guns as many as eight times each night.

To be able to react to calls for fire quickly, accurately and with the appropriate weight of fire, Field Gunners rely heavily on good communications, accurate survey and reliable meteorological information together with well–defined and known procedures. I believe our supported arms would agree that in most cases they got this response – there were the odd problems such as the Scots Guards' attack on Tumbledown being held up by a rogue gun firing short – but it was achieved with very few of the normal aids one would expect to have. Meteorological data was given out by HMS *Fearless* on a daily basis but was of very limited value and far from what we expect for gunnery purposes. The only sensible way to overcome this problem was for the FOOs to fire at a known point on the map and then deduce the meteorological corrections that should be applied in that local area. This was fine by day but impractical by night. Another must for consistent and accurate fire is good survey. To concentrate accurately the fire of dispersed batteries demands that they should all be on the same survey state. This was impossible to achieve because of the lack of adequate survey equipment or mobility, but was overcome by FOOs adjusting individual batteries on to the target. On many occasions, however, it was necessary to accept the dispersion of fire.

One particular difficulty throughout the campaign was the inadequacy of our communications. Not only were there insufficient secure radios, which meant that the Divisional Artillery Command Net was insecure, but we were unable to run a technical net over which all technical data is passed. Hence I was unable to command the Close Support Artillery in the normal way. As is stated earlier this responsibility was devolved to Commanding Officers

Setting up a Rapier surface-to-air missile battery above San Carlos Water.
Soldier: Magazine of the British Army

but made more difficult by the two Close Support Regiments being on two different types of radio set – one operated on High Frequency (HF) sets and the other on Very High Frequency (VHF) sets. This problem was overcome by exchanging Liaison Officers, with radios, between the two Regiments.

To date I have not mentioned Blowpipe. This is a portable, hand–held, air defence system which is used for local air defence. They are very cumbersome and difficult to carry and as a result many launchers and missiles were damaged in being moved either by helicopter or by marching troops. However, the greatest difficulty with this system is that, on being distributed amongst the Commandos and battalions, there were problems in siting them. Too few of the supported arms' commanders were aware of their capabilities and limitations and too many of them were unused to thinking sufficiently of the air threat. This latter point was quickly erased with experience gained but even to the end few realized that Blowpipe is

A 105mm light gun prepares to fire on Sapper Hill during the final advance on Stanley. *Soldier: Magazine of the British Army*

designed to attack 'head on' targets rather than 'crossing' targets. Needless to say, the latter category were in the greater numbers with the result that Blowpipe came under some severe, but often unwarranted, criticism.

My remit has been to tell how the Royal Artillery tackled the problems confronting it during the campaign and this is, I hope, what I have achieved. However, in doing so, I may have given the impression that our problems were overwhelming and the campaign was a long series of frustrations for us. This was certainly not the case. I believe we met the challenges as they arose and learnt from them. Whilst we were disappointed with some aspects of our performance it is very clear that we played a vital part in the successful retaking of the Falkland Islands. Indeed the enemy commander, Major–General Menendez, is reputed to have said 'Your infantry won the battles but it was your artillery that won the war.'

Advance Force Operations: The SAS

Major-General Michael Rose (Commanding Officer, 22nd Special Air Service Regiment, Falklands War)

The Falklands War was the first large–scale amphibious operation in which the 22nd Special Air Service Regiment had taken part since World War II. Nevertheless, despite the period of 40 years which had intervened, both D and G Squadrons of the SAS were successfully able to carry out the wide variety of tasks given to them because of firm adherence to the original principles established in 1941 by David Stirling, the founder of the Regiment. Since the war, the Regiment had also gained world–wide experience in limited war operations – most notably through its involvement in counter–terrorist operations in Northern Ireland. Consequently, without any time needed for preparatory training, SAS soldiers were in a position to accept the surrender of South Georgia only 23 days after its capture by Argentine forces. In addition SAS patrols were able to deploy on to the Falklands within four weeks of the original invasion of the islands, where they were able to sustain effective operations behind enemy lines for a continuous period of 45 days.

Only two months before the invasion of the Falkland Islands, Regimental Headquarters, who were continually reviewing contingencies around the world, had been assured by a superior headquarters that no scenario could be envisaged where it would be necessary to deploy the SAS to the Falkland Islands. In retrospect, the classic SAS offensive and intelligence–gathering roles which they carried out against the Argentine forces were to prove central to the successful conduct of the war. With the benefit of hindsight, it is possible to state that without the contribution of the SAS,

the war could not have been won in the way that it was, i.e. in so short a time frame and with so relatively few casualties. It is a demonstration of the quality of the SAS soldier that everything that was achieved by the SAS was done in the face of the highest number of casualties taken by the Regiment since World War II, when the loss of a helicopter cost the lives of 20 of the finest and most experienced soldiers in the Regiment.

Planning for the deployment of the SAS started on 2 April 1982, which was the day that the Falkland Islands were invaded. D Squadron, which was on standby for operations world–wide, flew to Ascension Island on 5 April, where it embarked on RFA *Fort Austin*. Meanwhile the Commanding Officer arranged with the Brigade Commander of 3 Commando Brigade to embark his Regimental Headquarters

Walking wounded of the Scots Guards moving towards a Scout helicopter for evacuation. The figure on the extreme right can be recognised as a member of the SAS by the 5.56mm Armalite rifle he carries. *Soldier: Magazine of the British Army*

'Contact, Wait Out'. May 1982. Colour photolithograph after Peter Archer, published by the Royal Corps of Signals, 1984. *National Army Museum 8502–41*

on HMS *Fearless*. It was agreed that because the SAS were to provide much of the intelligence–gathering capability on land, it would be appropriate for them to operate under tactical control of the Land Force Commander rather than the naval Task Force Commander who was likely to be concerned largely with the sea and air campaign in the South Atlantic. Furthermore, SAS activities would need to be co–ordinated with those of the SBS, who had been given responsibility for beach reconnaissance and whose headquarters were also located on HMS *Fearless*. Meanwhile G Squadron was ordered to move to Ascension Island where it arrived on 20 April.

On 17 April, the Commander–in–Chief held a planning conference on Ascension Island at which time orders for Advance Force

Operations were given. Since it was the Commander–in–Chief's overall intention first to recapture South Georgia before proceeding with main operations on the Falkland Islands, the initial SAS plan envisaged D Squadron supporting operations in South Georgia, whilst G Squadron were to be responsible for reconnaissance operations throughout the East and West Falkland Islands. At this early point of the war, no information was available concerning deployments, strength, or morale of the Argentine forces on the Islands. It was clearly vital that this intelligence be obtained in order to allow proper plans to be drawn up for the recapture of the Islands. Once South Georgia had been recaptured, D Squadron was to be redeployed to the Falkland Islands in order to carry out offensive operations.

Four days later, on 21 April, 19 Troop D Squadron, who by now had been re–embarked on HMS *Antrim* and HMS *Endurance*, established a troop position on the Fortuna Glacier. This location was chosen because it was sufficiently remote from the Argentine garrisons, thought to be at Grytviken and Leith, for there to be no compromise during the insertion of the patrols by helicopter. It was the intention of the patrols to move across the Fortuna and Nuemayer Glaciers to positions from where observation of enemy positions could be established. Unexpectedly poor weather conditions prevented any movement across the glaciers, and 19 Troop were withdrawn from the Fortuna Glacier to HMS *Antrim* on 22 April. During the extraction of the patrols, two helicopters were lost – fortunately without loss of life or injury. That night, although weather conditions had not greatly improved, with some difficulty reconnaissance patrols from 17 Troop went ashore by boat and landed on Grass Island from where they were able to observe the enemy garrison at Leith. First intelligence reports indicated that the Argentine forces were not alert and spent most of the day indoors sheltering from the weather.

Following a successful attack by a naval helicopter against an Argentine submarine on 25 April, it was decided that a British landing force should be put ashore as soon as possible, supported by naval gunfire. Even though the main assault force from M Company Royal Marines had not yet reached South Georgia, it was decided to launch an immediate assault because it was clear that surprise had been lost and SAS reports showed that the defending Argentine garrison was not likely to put up significant opposition. The only troops available for the operation were those of D Squadron and a small advance party of the Royal Marines. The wisdom of this decision became apparent the next day when Grytviken surrendered to the landing force without offering any opposition. The actual surrender was taken by the Sergeant–Major of D Squadron!

While operations in South Georgia had been going on, G Squadron had been planning

View of Pebble Island after the SAS raid on the night of 13/14 May during which 11 Argentine aircraft were destroyed. *Courtesy of Major–General H M Rose*

to establish reconnaissance patrols on both East and West Falkland Islands. Since there was still no firm information available concerning the whereabouts of the Argentine forces, or how extensively they patrolled the Islands, it was decided to establish patrols covering all the main centres of population. These patrols would have to be landed at some distance from their targets to avoid compromise as the only available means of covert deployment was by Sea King helicopters of 846 Naval Air Squadron. Between 30 April and 2 May eight patrols of G Squadron and two patrols of the SBS were landed on the Falkland Islands. The information these patrols gained was invaluable. Argentine forces were concentrated mainly around Port Stanley, Darwin/Goose Green, and Mount Challenger on East Falkland, and in Fox Bay and Port Howard on West Falkland. The Argentine soldiers seemed ill–led, maintained a poor routine in defence, and appeared to be demoralized. Much of their time was spent looking for food. Most importantly, they did not appear to have any main defensive positions around San Carlos Water which was the proposed location of the main amphibious landings.

The G Squadron patrols communicated nightly with their Squadron Headquarters by radio, and moved their locations frequently to avoid detection by DF. Although the Argentine forces suspected a British presence on the Islands, by careful camouflage and by selecting unlikely positions all G Squadron's patrols were able to survive the great many searches mounted by Argentine patrols. Numerous Argentine positions were identified, including the location of the main military headquarters in Port Stanley, as well as the presence of a battalion group defending Darwin/Goose Green. Air attacks were mounted against many of these positions – the most important of which was an attack mounted by Harrier aircraft against an Argentine helicopter force on 20 May concealed to the west of Port Stanley.

This attack destroyed a significant proportion of their lift capability which constituted a major blow to General Menendez, who had planned to move his reserve troops by helicopter in order to block any British moves away from San Carlos Water. The loss of such an important number of helicopters meant that the Argentine forces no longer had strategic mobility, and this gave the British ground forces relative freedom of movement throughout the Islands.

Whilst G Squadron was establishing itself ashore in the Falkland Islands, D Squadron moved from South Georgia to HMS *Hermes*, where the headquarters of G Squadron was located. They immediately started to plan an attack on an Argentine satellite airfield on Pebble Island close to West Falkland from where many of the Pucara missions were being launched. On 11 May, a reconnaissance patrol from 17 Troop was inserted near Port Purvis, some 20 nautical miles from Pebble Island. Four days later the patrol had produced sufficient intelligence about enemy dispositions on the airfield for a Squadron raid to be planned. This was mounted from Sea King helicopters directly onto the airfield under cover of naval gunfire support from HMS *Glamorgan*.

Once D Squadron had established itself on the airfield, the enemy was engaged with mortar and machine gun fire. At the same time explosive charges were attached to the aircraft which were dispersed around the airfield. At first light D Squadron withdrew, having destroyed 11 aircraft on the ground. They suffered three minor casualties. This was the highest number of aircraft destroyed in a single operation by the SAS since the campaign in the Western Desert in 1942.

Three nights later, in an administrative move from one ship to another, a Sea King helicopter carrying elements of both G and D Squadrons crashed with the loss of 20 members of the Regiment, including both Squadron Sergeant–Majors.

Notwithstanding this appalling tragedy, the next night D Squadron flew to Darwin/Goose Green to mount a diversionary raid against the garrison in order to draw possible Argentine reinforcements away from San Carlos Water whilst the main amphibious landing was taking place. The operation succeeded well, and prisoners interrogated after the 2 Para capture of the settlement stated that they believed the raid to be the main landing. The next morning, whilst moving across country to join up with disembarked British forces, who by then had established themselves in San Carlos Water, D Squadron shot down a Pucara aircraft.

Meanwhile a G Squadron patrol had identified the fact that there were no firm enemy positions on Mount Kent. Being only ten miles to the west of Port Stanley, it was a vitally important feature in respect of the defence of the town as it dominated most of the Argentine defences. Thus, although Mount Kent was 40 miles from San Carlos Water, it was decided to reinforce the patrol position with the whole of D Squadron. The move was completed on 27 May. Once sufficient logistic assets had been put ashore in San Carlos Water, a battalion group would then be established on Mount Kent by 3 Commando Brigade with a view to securing positions for the final attack on Port Stanley. In the event it was not possible for 3 Commando Brigade to proceed with this operation until 30 May – by which time D Squadron had come under increasingly severe attacks from Argentine fighting patrols. On the night of 29 May two large Argentine special force patrols who were attempting to regain control of Mount Kent were ambushed. In the ensuing battle, which lasted all night, two enemy soldiers were killed and six captured at a cost of three men wounded. On 30 May Mount Kent was handed over to 42 Commando and D Squadron was withdrawn to San Carlos Water to prepare for subsequent operations.

Between 27 May and 10 June when the main battle started for Port Stanley, SAS pa-trols were active both in East and West Falkland. During this period, G Squadron cleared ground from Estancia House to the Murrell Heights and Mount Low which lie to the north of Port Stanley. This operation secured the left flank of 3 Commando Brigade for their main assault on Port Stanley which began on 11 June. On 5 June, D Squadron had deployed additional patrols to West Falkland, one of which was located in Fox Bay. Tragically, its position was identified by Argentine DF on 10 June, and its forward observation post surrounded. Ignoring orders to surrender, the

On 24 May reconnaissance patrols of D Squadron 22nd SAS were flown forward to occupy Mount Kent. They held it against enemy Special Forces and fighting patrols until 42 Commando could be landed by helicopter on the night of 30/31 May. *Courtesy of Major–General H M Rose*

Troop Commander was killed and one soldier was captured in the ensuing battle. On 8 June the forward Regimental Headquarters of the SAS made contact with the Argentine Headquarters in Port Stanley in order to apply psychological pressure on the Argentine forces with a view to bringing about an early surrender. The British now held the high ground surrounding Port Stanley, and it was important that the battle for the Falkland Islands did not extend into the town. This would cause untold civilian as well as military casualties. It was therefore worth trying to get General Menendez to accept a formula involving an honourable surrender before such a battle became necessary. Although no assurances were given by the Argentine Staff Officer, Captain Barry Melbourne Hussey, with whom initial discussions took place, it was agreed that a line would be kept open between the two Headquarters. Each succeeding day, as the Argentine position became more hopeless, greater psychological pressure was put on the Argentine Headquarters by the SAS, via this open line.

The Commanding Officer SAS, and three soldiers, stand beneath the SAS Union flag beside Government House, 0700 hrs 15 June. The flag was previously flown on South Georgia.
Courtesy of Major–General H M Rose

On 12 June, D Squadron was moved to join G Squadron on the Murrell Heights and Mount Low. They were ordered to mount a diversionary raid across Heardon Water to the north of Port Stanley harbour in order to prevent the forthcoming main attack on Wireless Ridge being outflanked. The SAS raid,

which took place on the night of 13 June, was supported by rigid raiding craft of the Royal Marines, and although three minor casualties were sustained, it succeeded in drawing a significant amount of enemy fire away from 2 Para on Wireless Ridge. To the south of the island, a patrol of G Squadron had managed to infiltrate the enemy lines and had established themselves on Seal Point. Prior to, and during, the battle of Mount Tumbledown, this patrol was able to call down observed artillery fire from 4 Field Regiment Royal Artillery on the rear of the enemy positions. So great was the carnage caused that on the morning of 14 June, when the Argentine forces were fleeing from their positions, a voluntary halt was called by the patrol to the devastating artillery fire on the retreating enemy.

At 1100 hours on 14 June, the Argentine Headquarters contacted the SAS Headquarters, and invited a negotiating team to fly to Port Stanley to discuss a cease–fire on East Falkland. A small team comprising the Commanding Officer, a radio operator, and an interpreter from the Royal Marines, arrived in Port Stanley at 1300 hours, and after six hours of negotiations General Menendez was persuaded to surrender his sea, air, and land forces to the British throughout the entire Falkland Islands.

This account has concentrated solely on the SAS contribution to the Falklands War. It was stated at the outset that it was believed that the war could not have been won so speedily nor with so relatively few casualties without the contribution made by the SAS. It is, of course, even more true to state, and this needs no emphasis, that without the courage, determination and professionalism of the ordinary soldier, sailor and airman, the Falklands War could not have been won at all.

Unsung Heroes

Marion Harding (National Army Museum)

No military force can fight effectively without support. When the Prime Minister decided to dispatch a Task Force to a remote group of islands over 8,000 miles away, she and her advisers were well aware that this force would need sustaining and reinforcing out of all proportion to its size. This is where the Corps of the British Army would come into their own.

Corps of Royal Engineers

The traditional tasks of the Royal Engineers are many and varied. Sapper units, including Commando, Parachute, Field and Field Support Squadrons, were involved in every action of the campaign. Other specialist Sapper support included mapping, bomb disposal, and postal services.

San Carlos Water, May–June 1982. Royal Signals setting up a Satellite Communication dish, as Welsh Guards march past and unloading operations are carried out. Colour photolithograph after Peter Archer, published by the Royal Corps of Signals, 1983. *National Army Museum 8411–41*

The huge demand for updated maps was met by the Military Survey section, which also began work on a new technique of Digital Terrain Modelling to depict ground contours in relief. Within weeks 750,000 conventional maps had been provided in over 350 formats.

On Ascension Island the Sappers constructed a three and a half mile fuel pipeline to, and an Emergency Bulk Fuel installation on, Wideawake Airfield in support of RAF operations.

The Engineers were also hard at work as soon as they disembarked at San Carlos. Each of the landing beaches required a water point; command posts were dug, field defences constructed, beaches and exits improved and buildings checked for possible booby traps. Sappers took part in the patrol programme, one being seriously wounded as a result.

As the beach–head developed, a Harrier operating base was built and maintained, often under fire, and two Emergency Bulk Fuel installations constructed, each of which delivered, at peak demand, 40,000 gallons of aviation fuel per day. These two capabilities proved critical in enabling the Task Force to make the best use of its available helicopters and Harriers.

In the advance, the Sappers played their classic role of reconnoitring with the leading infantry and breaching minefields. Their first major action was with 2nd Battalion The Parachute Regiment at Goose Green where the Recce Troop cleared routes and fought as infantry throughout the battle: a Corporal was killed by machine gun fire early in the action. The mine–clearing operations in Goose Green provided the first valuable intelligence of the campaign concerning enemy mines. It was a highly dangerous and nerve–racking process, probing through the ground for mines, and a light–hearted account by Corporal A Iles from later in the campaign reveals how exposed and vulnerable the Sappers were:

Digging in behind Goat Ridge was almost complete when Troopie approached and explained that whilst the Scots Guards were taking Tumbledown, the Gurkhas were to move forward slightly to the rear, ready to advance on Mt William once Tumbledown had fallen. A Coy were to lead around the north side of the mountain, to set up covering fire for the rest of the battalion during the assault. It was known, from intelligence, that there was a minefield on their planned route. They needed a section from the troop to lead them and I had been given the task. 'Can we take our trenches with us Sir?' I asked.

We moved off from the base of Goat Ridge at approximately 0300 hours. Myself and Spr Seth Roose were leading (he had the white handkerchief!). The Gurkha recce element were 15–20m behind and the rest of the section, under L/Cpl Shankland, in immediate reserve. We made good ground over the first 800m and were still 200m from the start of the minefield, but then I experienced a coldness I have never felt before. We had come close to a bird's nesting place and they let us know it with a hissing sound. Seth and I hit the ground, fingers tightening on the safety catch. We honestly thought that it was the enemy saying 'psst'. It took us some time to come back down to earth. Pushing on, we came to the start of the minefield. With a bit of patience we managed to find a safe route around it. Meanwhile, the battle for Tumbledown was going on. The Scots Guards had taken the first part of the ridge and were moving on to the centre.

Another traditional combat engineer task is bridge building and repair. The partially demolished bridge at Fitzroy was reconstructed using salvaged local scrap, and the Murrell Bridge replaced by an airportable bridge delivered and positioned by helicopter.

In the meantime, many critical Explosive Ordnance Devices tasks were carried out by bomb disposal engineers, both in the unfamiliar surroundings of Royal Navy ships and afterwards, ashore, clearing unexploded bombs and ammunition. Two bomb disposal engineers were killed attempting to defuse a bomb aboard *Antelope*.

The Royal Engineers Postal and Courier Service provided official and private mail services for the Task Force at sea and ashore, handling up to two tons of airmail daily and 1,000 bags of parcels each week. On the way south, the only opportunity available to the troops to send mail home was at Ascension Island, but mail was dropped to them from aircraft. Postal units followed the troops ashore and established themselves at Ajax Bay and San Carlos, then as the advance progressed they pressed forward, ending the campaign at Teal Inlet and Bluff Cove.

After the surrender a Military Works Area was established and major reconstruction work started. The Royal Engineers restored water and electricity to Stanley, repaired Stanley airfield, and provided accommodation. The full extent of the Argentine minefields had not been appreciated and their clearance produced a major problem which has not been entirely resolved to the present day.

Royal Corps of Signals

Good communications are the essence of warfare both at close range, and, as was the case with the Falklands War, at a distance of 8,000 miles. The land forces were mainly equipped with the Clansman range of man–portable radios. There are nine different radios in the group, three high frequency, five very high frequency and one ultra high frequency: some units received them for the first time just prior to embarkation. A satellite detachment of the Royal Corps of Signals at Ajax Bay provided communications with the UK throughout the whole campaign.

The site chosen for the landing, San Carlos Bay, was militarily ideal – a deep–water port surrounded by dominating hills which, once captured, would be perfect for close ground and air defence, but from a communication viewpoint it was a nightmare, since the hills

would screen signals from the forward VHF low–power Clansman manpack patrols and detachments. This was overcome by bringing the HF radio nets into play once the VHF sets became screened and out of contact, and command and control were thus maintained.

The shorter range VHF radios, together with UHF ground–to–air and ship–to–shore equipments, were primarily used to control the amphibious landings, the logistic build–up on land, and the immediate defensive perimeter, whilst HF radios became essential for the longer ranges to forward reconnaissance troops, artillery observation posts and other forces expanding out of the bridgehead.

The sheer volume of signals traffic was one of the most striking features of the campaign, ranging from press reports to operational orders. Captain J E Thomas described some of the variety of their work:

That evening we were joined by Alan Percival from MOD PR, who, in order to speed up the dispatch of press reports, came directly to check their scripts before transmission when possible. He was distinctive in his deer–stalker which remained on his head with and without a steel helmet. Press reports started to flow, in fact Robert Fox's vivid description of the Goose Green episode was passed over the cct.

Message traffic soon built up, eventually rising to about 500 messages a day over a single cct. Sig Jock Milne turned to me on receipt of yet another flash, saying that in training his instructor had gone through flash signals stating that they were unlikely to see one in their career. That day he handled 33! There was a bottle neck of low precedence traffic at our location due to the limitations of a Simplex 321Z station, this was compounded even more after the arrival of 5 Bde.

Men of the Royal Signals were among the first British troops to land on South Georgia and the Falklands: 264 Signal Squadron (SAS) provided the vital HF communications for the

SAS and SBS who were gathering intelligence behind Argentine lines. In addition, the Corps established a Communications Centre on Ascension Island and rear links for the infantry units. Also ashore were Air Support and Mobile Air Operations Team detachments equipped with Snowcat over–snow vehicles which were used to transport the heavier equipment.

Army Air Corps

656 Squadron Army Air Corps, affectionately known to some as 'Teeny Weeny Airways', operated six Westland Scout and six Westland–built Aerospatiale Gazelle helicopters in the Falklands: the Scouts were fitted with SS–11 wire–guided missiles. They flew day and night, in all weather conditions, providing vital battlefield communications, resupply and casualty evacuation. Their small size and manoeuvrability enabled the helicopters to carry out their tasks in areas where larger support helicopters would have been too vulnerable. A battlefield routine of 'ammunition in – casualties out' was soon established and an estimated 400 casualties were evacuated from forward positions. The Scout normally carried a crew of two; while the pilot concentrated on flying the aircraft, the aircrewman tended the wounded, and many lives were saved. A vivid picture of the risks of the 'casevac' operations was provided by Captain Jeff Niblett:

Some two kilometres down the track I suddenly saw two Pucaras diving out from the cloud base. Almost immediately they saw us and broke left to commence firing runs against us. I ordered a break and then began the most frightening few minutes I have ever experienced. As the Pucaras saw us break so they took one of us each and commenced attacks on us. The featureless terrain was a perfect killing ground for the fixed wing and afforded us no cover at all.

My air gunner, Sgt Glaze, was by now frantically leaping about the cabin area passing details of the runs against us. Using the ground to best advantage and no doubt restricted themselves by the low cloud base, they ran at us from every conceivable direction, at all heights, a variety of speeds and firing a combination of their deadly weaponry – rockets, cannon and machine guns. Within a minute, both Pucaras turned against my aircraft and what had previously seemed an insurmountable problem became nigh–on impossible. However, our evasion manoeuvres were successful and we eventually managed to work our way towards Camilla Creek House where we believe small arms fire drove them off.

As they turned and ran I made a dirty dash for safety by the only hedge for miles, carried out my fastest ever shut–down and ran for the nearest fox–hole – almost overtaking my air gunner in the process. Our overwhelming relief in having survived was shattered when we suddenly learnt that the other Scout had been shot down.

Three Scouts were detached to 3 Commando Brigade in support of 2 Para and took part in the attack on Darwin and Goose Green, mainly in the casualty evacuation role. The detachment then rejoined the main body of 656 Squadron whose Scouts spearheaded the successful heliborne assault on Swan Inlet on 2 June. On 7 June at Egg Harbour House on Lafonia, SS–11 missiles were fired at an enemy patrol during the deployment of observation post parties from 1/7th Gurkha Rifles and eight Argentine infantrymen armed with anti–aircraft missiles captured.

During the attacks by the Scots Guards and 1/7th Gurkha Rifles on Mount Tumbledown and Mount William, helicopters from 656 Squadron evacuated casualties under fire, moved observation post parties and replenished combat supplies from their base at Fitzroy Settlement, though their fuel supplies ran dangerously low at times. The Squadron also

3 Para Regimental Aid Post at the rear of Mount Longdon. Casualties are being transferred from over–snow vehicles to a Scout helicopter for evacuation to a Forward Dressing Station. *Express Newspapers/Airborne Forces Museum*

engaged enemy guns defending Port Stanley with SS–11 missiles.

Royal Army Chaplains' Department

As soon as the Task Force sailed, the five members of the Royal Army Chaplains' Department who accompanied it began organizing regular Church services, padre's hours and informal discussion groups. These were well received from the outset, but the further south the troopships sailed the less optimistic everyone became that the Argentines would withdraw without fighting and the more did thoughts of what was impending impinge on their minds: it was to the chaplains that they turned to express their innermost hopes and fears. A daily slot on the ship's radio system was therefore provided for them and they under-

took the writing of a regular 'Thought for the Day' for the ship's daily broadsheet, as well as transcribing BBC World Service news bulletins for publication.

Once the Task Force landed at San Carlos, the ministry of the chaplains acquired a different emphasis. Periods of intense activity alternated with periods of waiting, foul weather conditions, and the constant threat of enemy air attack or counter–attack took their toll on the soldiers' nerves; the chaplains were there to provide encouragement.

When the wounded started coming in to the Regimental Aid Posts, doctors and medical staff were appreciative of the pastoral support afforded to them and the wounded – after the battles there was the necessary duty of burying the dead, both British and Argentine, and of offering comfort to those whose close friends had been killed in action. There were also letters to be written and procedures to be followed regarding the next–of–kin and for the support of those who had the difficult task of looking after the bereaved at home.

The part played by the Royal Army Chaplains' Department in bolstering the morale of the forces should not be underestimated. Shortly after returning from the conflict The Reverend David Cooper, who accompanied 2 Para throughout the fighting, described how the presence of death brought many soldiers to examine their religious beliefs:

About my own feelings, when it seemed that I just might be killed, the thought that was uppermost in my mind was not the fear of death, it was the sadness and anguish it would cause to people whom I love and who I hope love me and that, I think, was my chief thought. I think it was probably true for a lot of other soldiers as well. I remember one lad poking his head out of a depression that was all of three inches deep and I was in one next to him that was about four inches deep, after a particularly heavy spate of shelling, and he said, 'Well, I tell you what Sir, after this I am going to be confirmed. I have learned more about myself in the last ten minutes than I have ever known in my life.' I think that was probably true of most people. By now, of course, the tissues are growing over the scars though I hope they will remember just what they did say when they were faced with death. I didn't expect to survive and I am amazed now how I did live. I remember when I was with four stretcher bearers and we were about to cross a hedge when all of a sudden it was just shot up around me. It just ceased to exist and how on earth any of the lads around me managed to survive I will never know. And so, when we got to Stanley it became important to me that we should mark our safe arrival as soon as possible. I had promised the soldiers that we would have a service in Stanley Cathedral as soon as we could and we did. I think that service was important for all the soldiers and I think the Chaplain was important to them for what he represents.

Royal Corps of Transport

The Royal Corps of Transport was involved in the daunting job of moving the Task Force with its vehicles, ammunition and operational equipment from the outset of the campaign. For most of the first week in April supplies were transported by road, and to supplement its own vehicles the Corps chartered about 100 civilian 40ft flat–bed trucks. Territorial Army vehicles and drivers were fully utilized over the first weekend. 39,108 tons of freight were moved by road alone. From the second week the RCT employed British Rail facilities, 44 special trains being hired.

Specialist advice in loading shipping, much of it commercial, and detachments on the Royal Fleet Auxiliaries and merchant ships which sailed with the Task Force, was provided by 17 Port Regiment. The Regiment also supplied two detachments to each of the Landing Ships deployed, one consisting of Port Operators or stevedores, and the other as crew for the 126ft, powered Mexeflote rafts, each of which could carry 55 tons of stores. The lack of shore–based berthing facilities in the Falklands meant that the Mexeflotes had a vital role to play in transporting men and supplies ashore at San Carlos, Bluff Cove and Teal Inlet; they also carried out an enormous amount of cross–decking at Ascension. One of the raft commanders, Corporal A E Dimmick, gave some idea of the variety of functions the raft fulfilled:

Mexeflote was used in so many ways too numerous to mention. Apart from our main job of logistic support, the rafts were used as helicopter landing pads, buffers between ships, and platforms, so that work could be done on the damaged ships. My raft was used to repair the ill fated RFA Sir Galahad *which had an unexploded bomb on board before Bluff Cove. The thought of the bomb going off never entered our minds for it was a job which had to be done.*

We left 'Bomb Alley' and moved around to

a forward position to unload vital supplies; mine was the only raft involved and the place was Teal Inlet. My Mexeflote, just 66' long and capable of carrying 55 tons, worked solidly for two weeks, sometimes carrying up to 100 tons of 105mm ammo to the shore; the raft most of the time up to 2 foot under water. The men were split into two teams working 18 hour shifts. The raft was holed, damaged and in one instance nearly sank but we bailed out, welded up and carried on.

Of equal importance was the RCT's involvement at airports. Movement Control Check Points were established at all the ports being used, at RAF Brize Norton and RAF Lyneham, and in most unit lines. The Air Monitoring Centre at South Cerney in Gloucestershire processed, accommodated and moved troops to air–heads.

Deployed on Ascension Island, in HMS *Fearless* and in support of 38 Group RAF, were some 50 personnel of 47 Air Despatch Squadron. Prior to the availability of Port Stanley airfield great reliance was placed on the rapid aerial delivery of vital stores to the Task Force and the air crews flew many long sorties to drop supplies to the ships.

Elements of the RCT/RAF Joint Helicopter Support Unit were also deployed on Ascension, where a fleet of support helicopters ferried stores and passengers from the island to passing vessels. A small team of helicopter handlers were responsible for the movement of stores within the Task Force and for helicopter handling during the campaign.

Road transport on the Falklands was provided by 407 Troop which was attached to 5 Infantry Brigade. Because of the boggy condi-

'Bravo' Slipway, Port Stanley, after hostilities had ended. A Ramp Cargo Lighter is seen on the left and a Mexeflote Raft on the right.
Royal Corps of Transport Museum

tions, the unit was equipped with tracked Snowcats, normally used for over–snow movement in Norway.

The Army Medical Services

The work of the Army Medical Services did not begin only with the landing of the Task Force on the Falkland Islands. The importance of the 'self–help' element in the treatment of battlefield casualties had long been recognized and full advantage was taken of the long voyage south to ensure that, by the time they went ashore, all troops were thoroughly rehearsed in battlefield first aid. On board *Canberra* regular tutorials were held and films of Vietnam casualties shown to the medical staff. At a lower level, advanced first aid lectures and 'practicals' were organized for the

Trench–foot and frostbite cases from 3 Para sheltering in a woodshed at Teal Inlet.
Airborne Forces Museum

commandos and paratroops. Attention was also paid to the problems of survival in the bleak wastes and freezing temperatures of the Falklands, in particular the avoidance of trench–foot and hypothermia. In the event, the climate still took its toll: trench–foot was rife among those who waded ashore at San Carlos because of poor boots and icy conditions and, despite boiling and chlorinating all water, there were a

number of cases of diarrhoea, known as 'Galtieri's Revenge', which had a debilitating effect. Nor was the lesson of World War II that blood supplies are crucial to the success of battlefield surgery forgotten: on board *Canberra* alone 900 half–litre bags were willingly donated by the troops, an investment to which some of them were later to owe their lives.

The non–combatant status of the Medical Services does not invest its members with immunity to shot and shell. Their presence at the 'sharp end' of war is attested by the number of VCs which have been awarded for their selfless devotion to duty down the years. The Falklands campaign was no exception. Medical personnel of all ranks were to be found tending casualties under fire on the battlefield and in the Regimental Aid Posts and Field and Advanced Dressing Stations, all of which were vulnerable to enemy artillery fire and aircraft strikes.

One example of their gallantry will have to suffice: whilst 16 Field Ambulance was disembarking from *Sir Galahad* at Fitzroy Creek, Argentine aircraft attacked, killing the Second–in–Command and two soldiers, and wounding 13 others. Despite the loss of most of its equipment, in the next two hours, 16 Field Ambulance treated 135 casualties from the action. Only then did it attend to its own wounded. Warrant Officer A L Viner and Sergeant C P Forshaw were eyewitnesses of the scene:

At 1730 hrs two Skyhawk fighter bombers attacked the Sir Galahad *and* Sir Tristram *which was nearby. No warning was given. One large bomb ripped into the tank deck of the* Sir Galahad *and another into the accommodation decks. The ship was soon burning furiously and there was little to do but abandon ship. Somehow the troops made their way through the smoke and devastation to the main deck where the majority of medics were already busy treating injuries, while others decided to take to the rafts. On the main deck Sea Kings and Wessex helicopters were busy plucking troops from the burn-*

ing deck below. RSM McHale was trying to sort out the casualties into a system of priorities for evacuation whilst Sgt Naya was earning his MM for his actions in tending to the wounded.

Altogether, some 300 members of the Army Medical Services were deployed in the Falklands, including 30 Royal Army Medical Corps doctors and surgeons, four Royal Army Dental Corps dentists, ten non–medical RAMC officers, six Queen Alexandra's Royal Army Nursing Corps officers and 249 soldiers and servicewomen.

In the course of the campaign some 650 battle casualties were treated and 310 major operations carried out on land. Only three men subsequently died of their wounds, and no Briton died whilst ashore in the medical treatment chain. Though the exceptional fitness of the land forces undoubtedly played an important role in reducing casualties, the outstanding professional medical attention given to the wounded in the field, and later in the hospital ships and sick bays of the fleet, saved untold numbers of lives.

Corps of Royal Electrical and Mechanical Engineers

The Royal Electrical and Mechanical Engineers kept the Army's equipment operational during the Falklands campaign. The deployed force included the Workshop Squadron of the Commando Logistic Regiment, 10 Field Workshop of 5 Infantry Brigade, and the integral unit workshops, Light Aid Detachments and attached tradesmen. Major A D Ball of 10 Field Workshop travelled south with part of the unit on the *QEII*, where the journey–time was put to good use:

The time on board was spent on concentrated military training. Weapons were tested and zeroing checked by firing over the stern at floating gash bags; helicopter emplaning and

deplaning drills were rehearsed; a concentrated programme of first aid training, physical training and radio training was completed. Meanwhile, the operational plans were discussed and intelligence briefings held.

As far as our workload was concerned we had to support all the training which was taking its toll on units' equipment. Fortunately, we had had the foresight to get two of our airportable trainers loaded aboard QEII which gave us good telecommunications and small arms repair facilities; we used the ship's facilities for manufacturing tasks and although the ship's workshop was surprisingly limited, the engineering staffs were extremely helpful at all times. We designed and jointly manufactured Air Defence mounts for two .50in Browning machine guns; we attempted to make base plates for 81mm mortars but sadly failed; we fitted Turner winches to the Landrovers of the Brigade Signal Squadron and we repaired anything and everything that came our way. Regrettably, loading policy had prevented us taking full instrument repair facilities aboard and our ability to support instruments and office machinery was very limited; this was our only major weakness.

The Commando Workshop was distributed among a number of ships during the journey south and reassembled as a squadron in Ajax Bay on 28 May where it was initially deployed in the infantry role, in part responsible for the defence of the Brigade Maintenance Area. 10 Field Workshop arrived at San Carlos Bay on 3 June, where it deployed as Headquarters Beach Support area. Owing to shipping priorities much of the Workshop's stores were not unloaded, limiting its initial ability to operate. At this stage, however, the Commando Workshop was still able to cope with the workload, and 10 Field Workshop was used in the guarding of prisoners of war.

While 10 Field Workshop continued to build up its equipment and spares the pressure on Commando Workshop increased. The majority of the units landed and went into action without their integral workshops and tradesmen from Commando Workshop inevitably became involved in unit repairs. Forward Repair Teams were also deployed and an advanced Workshop Detachment established at Teal Inlet.

The Corps provided engineering support for the 27 helicopters of the Royal Marines Air Squadron and 656 Squadron Army Air Corps. The two Squadrons' Light Aid Detachments demonstrated considerable ingenuity in repairing battle–damaged aircraft and in overcoming spares shortages. Despite enemy action and the adverse environment, at no time were flying operations curtailed through poor serviceability.

Corps of Royal Military Police

The Royal Military Police detachment formed part of the Headquarters, 5 Infantry Brigade and comprised a captain, a platoon of General Police Duties non–commissioned officers and two Special Investigation Branch senior NCOs. It left Southampton on *Queen Elizabeth II* on 12 May and while on board its duties consisted of running a military information desk and providing discipline patrols around the ship.

On 2 June the detachment landed at San Carlos Bay where it was attached to Beach Logistic Control and, together with the Beach Master, was responsible for controlling all movement, including the marshalling of helicopters.

Captain A K Barley of the RMP describes the dangers of the first hours ashore:

> *During one of these periods we were attacked by the very fast, low–flying Skyhawk fighters. L/Cpl Cooper, who was closest to the action, needed little incentive to move quickly as he dived for the nearest trench. We were bombed on the beach–head but fortunately they did not find their targets. The missiles launched from* HMS Exeter, *operating in the sound, brought down two of the four Canberra aircraft in the attack.*

Nearly two weeks later, following the move to the Fitzroy/Bluff Cove settlements, they processed their first batch of prisoners of war. On the day following the operation to secure Mount Kent, they were augmented by 20 Royal Marine Police who assisted them to handle just over 80 prisoners. On arrival, the Argentines were taken to sheep–shearing sheds where the police strip–searched them and completed next–of–kin and capture cards. This done, they assisted British troops to guard the prisoners and helped a Tactical Questioning Team to 'weed–out' those believed to have useful information. Within the space of two days, about 350 prisoners from Mount Harriet and Two Sisters were similarly processed.

Ten hours after the Argentine surrender the Military Police arrived in Stanley, where they were horrified to find hundreds of Argentine soldiers roaming the streets, many of them still armed. Captain Barley encountered this unnerving scene:

> *The things we saw were, to say the least, somewhat hairy. Thousands of Argentine soldiers were walking about with loaded weapons. They had primed grenades hung from the waist belt. Many times we had cause to walk in 'bricks', as in Northern Ireland, for the first 24 hours .*

The following day, the soldiers were rounded up by the Royal Marines and shepherded to the airfield where the police assisted the marines to disarm them before beginning the mammoth task of searching them before they were sent home. This proved to be a slow process as many of the prisoners had looted property. At the final count, over 11,000 prisoners were processed and repatriated, leaving the Military Police in the possession of masses of loot.

The next task was to catalogue this property and to establish a civil complaints department. On 1 July they were able to start taking civilian statements of complaints in respect of the damage, looting and destruction they had suffered.

An officer of the Royal Military Police clears the weapons of Argentine conscripts after the surrender at Port Stanley. *Soldier: Magazine of the British Army*

This, and many other tasks to restore normality, kept the Royal Military Police detachment at full stretch until, a little over two months from embarkation, it was homeward–bound.

Royal Army Pay Corps

With the activating in April of No 8 Airportable Shadow Field Cash Office, a Paymaster was nominated from 5 Infantry Brigade with a remit to act as Force Paymaster and make all on–the–spot decisions as circumstances dictated. He was later confirmed as Task Force Paymaster and made responsible for funding all Land Forces – Royal Navy, Royal Marines, RAF, and Army. The major Army units of 5 Infantry Brigade and 3 Commando Brigade each had with them their integral Paymaster and a small team of Pay Staff.

The plan was to resupply in the field when Brigade Maintenance Areas and Forward Maintenance Areas had been established on the Falklands. Supplies of cash to meet these payments were only possible because of the ingenuity of Task Force Pay Staff.

When not employed on their own specific tasks, Pay Corps Staff were deployed where they were most needed. Captain Harry Quinn, the Paymaster attached to 2 Para on board the *Norland*, revealed how his staff gave direct support to the fighting troops:

By this time we were drawing close to the Falklands and rumour and speculation were rife. Then suddenly we got our battle orders, the only detail being the date/time of H hour. San Carlos was to be our destination and plans for disembarkation were produced. The Pay staff were to be used as guides within the darkened ship for the troops going ashore on D–Day. We were also tasked to move ammunition, batteries and rations from the cargo decks to the helicopter loading decks. The day before D–Day the whole convoy feigned an attack on Port Stanley, then headed round the North of East Falkland to Falklands Sound. We crept down the channel, past the Argentinian positions, ship darkened and silent. Suddenly the naval bombardment began. The assault had begun. The noise and excitement were unbearable. 2 Para were the first Battalion ashore. By daylight we had moved into San Carlos water with the rest of the invasion fleet, primarily to avoid the attentions of the Argentinian Air Force. That first day everyone spent moving ammunition and rations while the SQMS and I manned the Battalion radio net.

When the Battalion was in the Fitzroy/Bluff Cove area, three men were sent forward to act as stretcher–bearers and ammunition carriers. The Pay Team with 1st Battalion Welsh Guards were involved in securing, storing and delivering combat stores to the rifle companies in addition to local defence. One of their NCOs was attached to the Field Record Office where he prepared casualty and missing lists. Once the Argentines had surrendered at Stanley, the team was involved in the documentation, processing, and guarding of prisoners.

There are many reports of gallantry in the field on the part of RAPC officers and men. During the battle for Mount Longdon, a Staff Sergeant with the 3rd Battalion Parachute Regiment's Pay Team was told by a Platoon Commander to clear some Argentine trenches and sangars in their rear. Taking three men with him, the Sergeant cleared three or four positions, taking prisoner any Argentines still alive, and handed over his prisoners before clearing two more.

At the end of the campaign, the Corps was justified in its pride in proving the military as well as the technical skills of its members.

Intelligence Corps

The Falklands campaign will feature in Intelligence history as a classic example of the unexpected. Prior to the war intelligence gathering had been concentrated on those parts of the globe where a perceived threat had been identified: in the military mind, the Falkland Islands and its Dependencies were a low–risk area.

The Intelligence Corps' involvement began with the requirement to carry out rapid debriefs of the British civilian and military personnel who had been repatriated from South Georgia and the Falklands after the Argentine invasion. Its next task was to create, at short notice, a complete intelligence organization to support the Task Force.

The Corps was expected to provide the resources for supplying combat intelligence, both to troops on the ground and command staffs, which included additional intelligence staffs, linguists, tactical questioners, imagery interpreters, analysts, and electronic warfare operators, who were responsible for such tasks as the interception of radio traffic.

For a small Corps, which has no central pool or reserve for meeting such emergencies, this was a formidable task. The officers and soldiers deployed had to be drawn from many different establishments and units, and therefore had not previously worked together. All had to be collected, briefed, equipped and dispatched at very short notice. Captain A G Thomas recalled these early, hectic, days:

Northwood is a major Naval HQ with the expected proliferation of senior naval officers plus a significant RAF presence. General Moore had moved his RM HQ to Northwood and we, as it were, completed the set. We were based with the RM staff in the underground facility so graphically described in the National Press in May 1982. Integration into what was an enormously professional staff was quick and painless although some revision of vocabulary was neces-

sary. Inter–service rivalry was keen and differ-
ences in emphasis and procedures did lead to
occasional misunderstandings; but the urgency
of the task in hand meant that everyone did
finally pull in the same direction.

An example of the type of duties on which
members of the Corps were employed can be
provided by 81 Intelligence Section which
served as 5 Infantry Brigade's Intelligence Section throughout the conflict. Five weeks of
intense activity for the Section began on 2
April. By the following morning it had prepared a briefing on the Falklands and the
Argentine armed forces, and the 3rd Battalion
of the Parachute Regiment was given a presen-
tation that afternoon. From then until 5 Brigade left *Queen Elizabeth II* at South Georgia
such presentations and further research occupied much of the Section's time. One corporal
spent much of his time on board ship distribut-
ing the 50,000 maps in 81 Section's possession
to the other units in 5 Brigade.

Once ashore at San Carlos, the Section
commenced operating as the Brigade Intelligence Cell, initially in a house at Darwin and after
a few days dispersed in Land Rovers at Fitzroy.
Here, prisoners were questioned, the Skyhawks
and Mirages preparing to attack Fitzroy moni-
tored, and maps prepared and marked.

The representatives of the Corps exercised their skills at all levels, from tactical unit
to the highest command, and played an important part in the joint operation.

Army Catering Corps

During the assembly of the Task Force, units
were fed by their own cooks who, when not
actually producing food, were employed in
assisting with the preparations for war. After
embarkation, all chefs were required to take
part in the shipboard training programmes,
but volunteers from the Army Catering Corps

also helped to man the ships' galleys in
their off–duty time.

On arrival off the Falklands, the cooks
disembarked with their units and provided
valuable support in a variety of roles. When it
was possible to do so they cooked food – often
in appalling conditions. When circumstances
or the speed of the advance prevented any
centralized feeding arrangements they
'yomped' across country, shifted stores, carried weapons and ammunition, and, in one
instance, manned and fired a machine gun in
an infantry section. A number of them also
acted as stretcher–bearers. At the height of the
conflict, some 200 cooks were catering for
nearly 4,000 soldiers.

The end of hostilities brought with it a new
challenge for the Army Catering Corps. Two
Warrant Officers were tasked to solve the problem posed by the feeding of some 600 special–
category Argentine prisoners held at Ajax Bay.
Captain M R J Lowe described the rapid improvisation which was necessary:

Argentine prisoners eating mutton stew. The Army Catering Corps faced the task of feeding
them as well as the British forces. *Airborne Forces Museum*

The two Warrant Officers started with one
petrol burner and nothing else. Within two days
they had built ovens out of 44 gallon oil drums,
made a hotplate from airducting misappropri-
ated from the freezer plant, and set up a series of

Pauses in the action provided the troops with the opportunity to dry out sodden clothing and equipment. *Express Newspapers/Airborne Forces Museum*

boilers (again from oil drums) and burner lines, having obtained more petrol burners. We also used some of the Argentinian cook trailers. The Argentinians didn't really appreciate the British habit of officers not eating until after the soldiers had been fed, but they got better with practice.

Two points stand out clearly in this necessarily brief survey of the contribution of the Corps to the victory in the Falklands. The first is that all regarded themselves as soldiers first and foremost and only then as specialists in their various fields. All units took part, alongside the Commandos, Paratroops, Guardsmen and Gurkhas, in the intensive programme of physical fitness, weapon, disembarkation and other training which took place on the troopships on the way south; all of them had to be prepared to take their place in the firing line, and many of them did; most of them suffered some casu-

alties. The second point is the high degree of flexibility within the Corps, not only in their ability to make–do or improvise when equipment and materials were lacking, but in their adaptability in taking on and making a success of the wide variety of tasks which fell outside their normal duties. The Corps of the British Army are deservedly proud of their vital role.

I am grateful for permission to quote from the following journals:

The Sapper, Vol 20, No 11, October 1982, p 445

The Wire, Vol 36, No 5, September 1982, p 373

The Army Air Corps Journal, No 9, 1983, pp 19–20

Journal of the Royal Army Chaplains' Department, Vol 27, No 2, December 1982, p 14

The Waggoner, Vol 2, No 15, March 1983, p 21

The Army Medical Services Magazine, Vol 37, June 1983, p 9

Journal of the Royal Electrical and Mechanical Engineers, No 33, April 1983, p 8

Royal Military Police Journal, Vol 33, No 1, 1982, p 46

Royal Army Pay Corps Journal, Vol 23, No 164, Autumn 1982, p 169

The Rose and Laurel, Vol 10, No 5, December 1982, p 34

Sustainer, No 16, 1983, p 140

Typical selection of uniform and equipment worn or carried by infantrymen during the campaign. The items varied between regiments and many individuals also took private purchases. Left to right, back to front: bergen; sleeping mat; combat jacket; combat jacket quilted liner; waterproof jacket; cold weather cap; leather gloves; woollen gloves; combat trousers; arctic longjohns; wool jersey; waterproof trousers; sleeping bag; 1958 pattern webbing set; puttees; Self Loading Rifle 7.62mm L1A1; combat trousers quilted liner; shovel; respirator with case; decontamination kit; first aid field dressing; face veil; khaki flannel shirt; scarf; bayonet for 7.62mm SLR; mess tins; knife, fork, spoon; wool socks; polyester socks; waterbottle; steel combat helmet; spare scarf; regimental head–dress; rubber overboots; five magazines for SLR; underpants; spare combat trousers; ankle boots. *National Army Museum*

The Royal Army Ordnance Corps

Brigadier Anthony Welch (Officer Commanding, Commando Ordnance Squadron, Commando Logistic Regiment, Royal Marines, Falklands War)

The first Royal Army Ordnance Corps soldiers to set foot on Falkland Islands soil were members of the Commando Logistic Regiment Royal Marines reconnaissance party, who were seeking a land base from which to operate. The RAOC provides men for the Ordnance Squadron of the Regiment, which is responsible for the logistic support of the Royal Marines Commando Forces.

The Squadron had sailed from the United Kingdom on 6 April 1982, along with the Task Force, and had men distributed throughout the Fleet. The Squadron Headquarters was embarked in RFA *Sir Lancelot* but transferred to RFA *Sir Galahad* at Ascension Island. During the trip to the South Atlantic plans were drawn up for the support of 3 Commando Brigade, once it had established a beach–head on the Falklands. In essence, the plan was to use two Landing Ships Logistic (LSL), the *Sir Galahad* and the *Sir Percival*, to carry two days of combat supplies, each backed up by a further four days of supplies in RFA *Stromness* and some 16 days of ammunition for the Brigade in the P&O Car Ferry, MV *Elk*. The LSLs would lay close inshore and provide direct support to the troops on land. Once empty, they would replenish from RFA *Stromness* and MV *Elk*, which would be sheltering in comparative safety outside the Total Exclusion Zone, only coming close inland under the cover of darkness. This plan was thought to provide both flexibility and safety for the vital sinews of war.

During the stopover at Ascension Island, stock was redistributed among the ships to achieve the necessary mix and balance of supplies to fit this plan. Throughout the three–week voyage south from Ascension Island, the Squadron tested its procedures, even practising moving ammunition by human chain from the ships' hold to the flight deck.

At dawn on D–Day, 21 May, *Sir Percival*, *Sir Galahad* and *Stromness* sailed into San Carlos Water, along with the amphibious Task Force, to act as floating depots. MV *Elk*, with its 5,000 tons of ammunition, stayed in the TEZ. The Squadron began to unload combat supplies and vehicles the moment that anchors were dropped. All went well until about 1430 when the Argentine Air Force war planes made themselves felt. *Sir Galahad* took 13 separate attacks that afternoon and by the evening of D–Day it was realized that supply direct from the ships would not work.

Ajax Bay, on the western side of San Carlos Water, had been earmarked as a possible Brigade Maintenance Area. It had a good beach but a frontage of only 300 yards and a depth of about 600 yards. Into that tiny area had to fit the Field Hospital, 45 Commando Echelon, the Headquarters of the Logistic Regiment, the Workshops and Transport Squadrons, the Fields Records Office, the Satellite Communications Unit, the Beach Operating Unit and the Ordnance Squadron with its hundreds of tons of stores and ammunition. There was little space available, particularly as part of the area was covered with stone runs, rivers of granite boulders which cascade down the mountain sides.

A respite in the air attacks on 22 May gave hope that resupply from the sea could continue alongside the more conventional land–based operation. This hope was dashed when RFA *Sir Galahad* was hit by a 1,000 pound bomb which ended up 30 feet from 300 tons of ammunition but failed to explode. RFA *Sir Lancelot* was also hit and the embarked troops and crew of both ships, plus the crew of HMS *Antelope* which had sunk the day before, found themselves on the shore of the now extremely crowded Ajax Bay. There was no time or space for the Ordnance Squadron to prepare neat storage layouts or segregated ammunition stacks; they just received stock from the ships and issued it to the fighting troops 24 hours a day.

On 25 May the Argentine Air Force turned its attention to Ajax Bay. They dropped eight bombs, four of which exploded killing five men and setting light to a stack of ammunition. Luckily, the fire did not spread and the Argentines did not visit again. The battle for Goose Green started the following day, with the Squadron supplying mortar ammunition direct to the base plates and Milan missiles to the front line. Gazelle and Scout helicopters flew into landing sites at Ajax Bay and then direct to the battle, taking great risks and flying with great skill.

As a result of the 1975 Defence Review, the Petroleum Platoon of the Ordnance Squadron was designated to be a Reserve Army unit. This meant that the Squadron deployed to the Falklands without their Petroleum Operators and had to make *ad hoc* arrangements. Ten members of 81 Ordnance Company, who had deployed with the 2nd Battalion, the Parachute Regiment, were given hasty instructions and then ran the Emergency Refuelling Site at Port San Carlos for helicopters and Harriers. At Ajax Bay, after only ten minutes of instruction, Private Potter, whose Army engagement ran out the day the Task Force landed, operated the Brigade's Petrol Point single–handed, almost without sleep, until 5 Infantry Brigade

arrived. He received a Mention in Dispatches award for his efforts.

Meanwhile, 5 Infantry Brigade had set sail from England with 81 and 91 Ordnance Companies in support. The Brigade was usually supported by a TA company which was not allowed to deploy. 81 and 91 Companies found themselves rescaling at short notice whilst the Officers Commanding set about getting to know their new formation and the staff. 91 Company had the added difficulty of having to undergo some reorganization, dropping its stores platoon and taking on a bakery platoon, a laundry platoon and a NAAFI/EFI section. The two companies set sail in *Queen Elizabeth II*, MV *Baltic Ferry* and MV *St Edmund*. The number of Ships Taken Up From Trade (STUFT) was on the increase.

Guardsmen of 5 Infantry Brigade move forward from San Carlos while a helicopter brings up heavy equipment. *Soldier: Magazine of the British Army*

During 5 Infantry Brigade's trip south, a logistic plan was worked out with the Colonel AQ (Personnel and Logistics) of Headquarters Commando Forces. This plan called for all logistic stock, for both 3 Commando and 5 Infantry Brigades, to be treated as force assets; both brigades would be supported from Ajax Bay with *matériel* remaining on board ship as back–up supplies and to provide some dispersion of assets. 81 and 91 Companies would operate under command of the Commando Logistic Regiment Royal Marines and, apart from a small element ashore, most of the personnel would be distributed among the support ships. A new Company Order of Battle was worked out and the unofficial title of 81st/91st Ordnance Company (*QEII*'s Own) was adopted. The two Officers Commanding decided that, as two heads were better than one, they would have joint command of the new organization, and thus the first RAOC unit with two Officers Commanding came into being.

91 Company was the first to arrive at Ajax Bay and immediately took on the petroleum handling task from the hard–pressed Commando team. The supply of petroleum was becoming a nightmare. Few vehicles were taken to the Falklands as it had been rightly assumed that the roadless terrain would preclude their use, so very little thought had been given by the staff to fuel resupply. There was a shortage of jerricans and bulk fuel containers and, as already noted, a lack of trained manpower. It had been rapidly discovered that, in order to keep radios and Rapier anti–aircraft systems working 24 hours a day, a lot of fuel was needed, and most of it had to be transported to the top of some very steep hills. 91 Company took on this thankless task with a will, discovering fuel where none was meant to be, getting it to the storage tanks and then issuing it day and night to units and detachments spread far and wide.

81 Company were not far behind their comrades and soon were supporting the elements of 5 Brigade. They were not without their problems, as the hasty loading of ships in the United Kingdom meant that stock was in the wrong order for offloading and much time was lost sorting out the mess. A considerable amount of *matériel* had to be moved before the required combat supplies could be reached. Ashore, operations were hampered by a lack of mechanical handling equipment and the fact that the ground, at the back of the beaches, had been churned into a sea of mud.

3 Commando Brigade was moving towards Stanley by this time, and the supply lines were stretching out behind them. To help reduce the length of these lines, the Ordnance Squadron established a Forward Maintenance Area at Teal Inlet and stock was moved from Ajax Bay by helicopter and LSLs. Under the shadow of Mount Kent, a forward distribution point was set up at Estancia House. Life was made exciting by Argentine air attacks and the passing interest of one of our own units which was shooting Upland Geese to supplement its diet and failed to notice the camouflaged stacks of ammunition.

In the south, the forward units of 5 Brigade had reached the settlement of Fitzroy. As the lines of communication were now stretched over a distance of 60 miles and movement forward was restricted to either LSL, Landing Craft or helicopters, it was decided to move the Logistic Base from Ajax Bay to Fitzroy. The Officer Commanding the Ordnance Squadron was sent to Fitzroy to prepare for the reception of stock and personnel. He arrived at the settlement just after RFA *Sir Galahad* steamed into the bay with elements of the Welsh Guards and some 400 tons of ammunition and stores on board. She joined RFA *Sir Tristram* which was also moving forward supplies.

5 Brigade Headquarters was establishing itself in a shearing shed in Fitzroy when the Argentine Air Force struck again. In a matter of minutes, *Sir Tristram* was crippled and *Sir Galahad* was ablaze. All efforts were turned to rescuing the troops and crew on board the ships and to tending the injured. Within an hour, the Argentine planes were back again, this time attacking the troops on the ground. For the second time in the conflict, logistic plans had to be abandoned and it was back to the drawing board.

Although *Sir Galahad* was terribly damaged and eventually scuttled, *Sir Tristram* was less badly hit. The fires on board were extinguished and it was found that the stores and ammunition in the holds were unaffected. Royal Engineers blew off the jammed rear door to the tank deck to allow a detachment of 81 Company on board to recover the stores. The bulkhead of

A helicopter assists in the transfer of men and stores of 5 Infantry Brigade from *Queen Elizabeth II* to *Canberra* at Grytviken, South Georgia. *Canberra* took the Brigade to the landing site at San Carlos. *Soldier: Magazine of the British Army*

81 Ordnance Company ration dump at Fitzroy a few days after *Sir Galahad* and *Sir Tristram* were bombed. Living conditions were spartan. *Courtesy of D Langham*

the tank deck was still hot to the touch and the wheels of the mechanical handling equipment smoked as they were driven in and out of the hold to remove the *matériel* and ammunition.

Back at Ajax Bay, it was decided that resupply would continue from the base there with just forward detachments remaining at Teal Inlet and Fitzroy. The air attacks on San Carlos Water and Ajax Bay had ceased but this local respite could not be guaranteed elsewhere. The long move forward of combat supplies, with helicopters flying hour after hour with underslung loads, continued sometimes direct to gun positions and sometimes to the forward logistic bases. As the guns moved ever closer to Stanley so the ammunition left behind them had to be picked up and moved to the new positions. Everyone steeled themselves for the final assault on the little town of Stanley.

Then suddenly it was all over; the Argentines had surrendered. There were feelings of disbelief, of relief, but very little of joy. Everyone was extremely tired and knew that, for the logisticians, the war was by no means over.

As the victorious troops entered Stanley, plans were being made for the resupply of the Task Force. The supply chain was to be the reverse of the one that had been operating up until this point. Its base was to be in Stanley, in the liberated Falkland Islands Company offices, and the outstations at Fitzroy, Teal Inlet, Ajax Bay, and across Falkland Sound at Fox Bay.

As the airfield at Stanley was not in a fit condition to receive transport aircraft, the first priority was to set up an organization to handle parachute–dropped stores and equipment. The second priority was to achieve some order in the chaos that was Stanley. Filth had to be cleared up so that storage and living areas could be created, piles of ammunition and weapons had to be checked for booby–traps and then made secure. The unloading and loading of ships, which had sailed round from San Carlos Water, had to be co–ordinated and, not least, the thousands of Argentine Prisoners of War had to be fed and watered. If anything, the peace brought more work than the closing days of the war.

Eventually, the time came for the Ordnance Squadron to leave for home. 81 and 91 Companies were to stay on for a few more weeks, with the main body departing on Friday 13 August by Hercules aircraft – a very good day despite the inauspicious date. The logistic task in the Falklands was handed over to the Falkland Islands Logistic Battalion, a new unit formed to support the post–conflict Garrison. Its Supply Company was to be the direct descendant of the units that served through the war and many of its officers and men were, over the next ten years, to be the same soldiers who had worked so magnificently to give the fighting troops the tools to finish their task.

The Legacy

Major–General Sir David Thorne (Military Commander, Falkland Islands and Dependencies, July 1982-August 1983)

The end of the war left a massive task of rehabilitation and construction in the Falkland Islands. At the same time, over the horizon to the west lay Argentina, an enemy defeated but with whom hostilities had not ceased. A highly professional defence was required, even at this nadir of Argentine fortunes. The Islanders were in a state of exhaustion and shock, although overjoyed at the outcome of the war. The Islands were strewn with the detritus of battle. Those servicemen who had fought the war needed to return home, but the task of securing the peace, and making good the chaos which existed, now had to be faced immediately and vigorously. It was midwinter in the Falkland Islands, communications with the outside world were tenuous, and the supply chain was 8,000 miles long.

Against this, the task of the Services, as given to me as Military Commander in early July 1982, was to provide for the protection of the Falkland Islands and Dependencies (South Georgia), and to assist in the rehabilitation of the region. What follows is an account of how the Army, in close concert with the other Services (including the Merchant Marine), carried out these tasks in the immediate aftermath of war.

To comprehend the extraordinary nature of the task it is necessary to sketch out the scene as found by the servicemen arriving to take over from those who had gloriously won back these Islands, 'where a garrison must be kept in a state that contemplates with envy the exiles of Siberia; of which the expense will be perpetual, and the use only occasional' (Samuel Johnson, 1733).

The situation, for those arriving by air, immediately spoke for itself. The airfield was operational but under extreme pressure. The calm, strong hand of Group Captain W J Wratten was in evidence, and essential. A battered airfield reception and air traffic control building, and across the runway the wind-blown tents of the Harrier Squadron commanded by Wing Commander P T Squires DFC, left little doubt of the difficulties ahead. The road to Stanley, already showing signs of excess wear, was littered with enemy weapons, equipment and ammunition in disorderly heaps. Stanley itself had suffered from a total swamping of its infrastructure; power, water and sewage services had all collapsed in the face of excess demand. There was no effective bakery or laundry, and accommodation was in such short supply that most servicemen were living on board the ships in the harbour. The stores were also, in the main, afloat, but there was no proper pier or unloading point. With weather conditions such that it was not always possible to get from ship to shore, it is little surprise that the main accommodation ship, the *Rangatira*, was nicknamed 'Rangatraz'. All around Stanley, and in various places throughout the Falklands, lay poorly marked or unmarked minefields, and in excess of 3,000 tons of ammunition in various states of safety. In the cemeteries at Stanley lay hastily–buried Argentine dead, and, on Mount Tumbledown and beyond, other Argentine soldiers lay in their trenches where they had fallen. Rehabilitation of the Islands was to present a massive task.

Meanwhile, the way in which an effective 24–hour defence of the region was to be carried out in the future had to be agreed before much construction work in the round could begin. At the same time, a tri–service headquarters had to be established immediately under the able hand of Colonel Roger Wheeler. The School House in Stanley provided the accommodation, and the satellite communication dishes were already in place to provide the shore–based link with the Ministry of Defence. A start had been made before we arrived, but a new staff team now needed to be created.

The first few days for this new team were to be crucial. It was necessary to report to the Chiefs of Staff about force levels, and then to create a concept of operation for the long–

success by the Argentines would have an extra, particularly damaging, effect on the confidence and perception of both the local inhabitants and the British public. The Argentine was only 400 miles away and the Islands covered an area the size of the Lebanon or Wales. The residents lived on the edges of the Islands; there were no roads outside Stanley, and, most significantly of all, the weather conditions could quickly limit or stop altogether any helicopter movement. In the main, movement on land could only be made on foot, by horse or cross–country vehicle. The usual option was to go by helicopter or by sea. The concept which was decided upon required a strongly defended strategic air and sea reinforcement point and operational base at Stanley, a central, forward

Stanley airfield, August 1982. The Sappers and other units manning and working to repair the airfield had to contend with atrocious weather conditions.
Courtesy of Major-General Sir David Thorne

term future. There were compelling political, financial and social reasons for reducing the land–based garrison to less than 2,000 men. Inevitably there were also military analysts who felt that corners could reasonably be cut. But hostilities had not ceased and any military

operating, alternative base at San Carlos/Port San Carlos, where ships, support helicopters, and reserves of ammunition could be positioned under Rapier air defence cover, and company bases at Stanley, Goose Green, Fox Bay, and Port Howard. Each company base would need helicopter refuelling facilities plus an immediate reserve of ammunition, water and food. Lastly, the integrated nature of the force was crucial to limiting the force levels, and an element of risk was inevitable. What we had to establish was the minimum credible force level, know precisely why, and then justify this in a dialogue with a cost–conscious, albeit generally helpful and sympathetic, Ministry – 8,000 miles away. The plan had to be sustained throughout a lengthy period of creation, during which we also had to establish an operational system, stay immediately ready 24 hours a day against the possible resumption of hostilities, and sustain spirits in an environment where the climate was a constant potential enemy and boredom was a threat to morale. Meanwhile there was high media interest, and the Argentines, some of whom burned with longing to regain their honour, were 45 minutes flying–time away.

This concept, based initially on force levels of 4,500 on land, reducing to around 3,200 once the Royal Engineers had done their work, was to be a constant source of testing discussion with all the visitors who came down to see for themselves the realities on the ground. Through many vicissitudes over the coming months, this plan stood firm. The scheme behind this concept was, while remaining acutely aware of financial, social, and political factors, to ensure that if servicemen had to fight, they would believe objectively that they were in with a good chance of success. But there was genuine concern that force levels would swamp the native inhabitants and eventually drive them away from their homes, thus creating defeat out of victory. It was for this reason, and with Sir Rex Hunt's encouragement, that a monthly chat with the Islanders on the Falkland Islands Broadcasting Station (FIBS) was instituted. The first talk was particularly important because in it the broad principles of the attack on the host of problems were spelt out:

- Force levels would be unlikely to reduce much, if at all, in the coming year

- We would rebuild the airfield first, and then the accommodation would be built

- We would clear areas of mines and booby–traps that were a threat to safety or were too restrictive to everyday life, and would isolate the remainder by fencing them in

- Already we had established, by careful discussion with settlement managers and local officials, where the camps could best be placed

- Our policy would be to position the camps just down the road from settlements (one or two miles, not 30 miles away); available and supportive – but not on top of the community

- We were fallible but disciplined: we respected property; and we were conscious of the need to respect and change as little as possible their former way of life

These and later talks were important; the need to be in tune with the Falkland Islanders was fundamental to ultimate success. The great heave, which was to last for nine months, had now begun. It was a situation where all materials and means for living, fighting, building and maintaining, had to come from the United Kingdom by air or sea, and be offloaded to be carried within the Falklands by Mexeflote or helicopter, save for a small area around Stanley. Tri–service co–ordination was critical and the performance of the Merchant Marine was also central to success. While the warships in the Falkland Island Protective Zone, the Harriers from the airfield, the Rapier detachments round Stanley and San Carlos, and the infantry at various locations, kept guard around the clock,

Erecting shelters, Stanley. Once the war was over there was an urgent requirement for accommodation for both men and stores. *Courtesy of Colonel P C R Howes*

the main thrust–lines of concurrent action to create the new structure and rehabilitate the Falklands became apparent.

Within three months 60,000 tons of stores were brought ashore (100,000 tons in nine months) and distributed round the Islands without any real port facilities. To achieve this, the Port Squadron worked virtually 24 hours a day, often in appalling weather conditions, including constant high winds; and the helicopter crews matched this dedication all the way as they uplifted essential materials to places where no vehicle would travel.

The most urgent target was the airfield. In what has been described as one of the largest single British military engineering tasks since World War II, the Royal Engineers, under the perceptive leadership of Colonel Derek

Brownson, first repaired and strengthened the Stanley airfield runway and then extended it sufficiently to accept Phantom aircraft. In mid–August the airfield was closed for 14 days to allow us to take the first major step of laying special matting along the 4,100 feet to upgrade the existing runway. The task was carried out with great skill and determination, in bitterly cold conditions. By 28 August the airfield was open again, and we could observe with satisfaction that we had maintained the supply of emergency spares and mail by use of air–drop and pick–up techniques from C–130s, a system not used in earnest since Borneo in the mid–1960s. Indeed, the Hercules force was a vital link in those early days, and they performed with exceptional skill. The 2,000–foot airfield extension then gradually gathered momentum. We were having intense teething problems in the quarry with both the rock drills and the rock crushers: a combination of exceedingly hard rock, constant harsh weather conditions and heavy rains created daily difficulties, but we pressed ahead. Arrestergear and all of the sophisticated facilities needed for fast–jet operations were installed, massive amounts of rock were quarried, crushed, laid and levelled, AM2 matting was laid with advice from our US friends, and on 16 October the first Phantom aircraft landed, piloted by Wing Commander Ian McFaddyen RAF. The Phantom air defence squadron now flew in over the next ten

A view of Stanley airfield with the inner harbour in the background, August 1982. The airfield was closed for 14 days in the middle of the month so that the runway could be repaired and lengthened with the use of metal matting. *Courtesy of Major–General Sir David Thorne*

days – testing for the first time our new runway of 6,100 feet of AM2 (US) matting. Drills had been practised, and the Argentines had tested the Falkland Islands Protective Zone (FIPZ) by flying at it. At this stage Rear Admiral Derek Reffell and the aircraft carrier *Illustrious* departed. The tri–service force now consisted of:

Navy

- at least one submarine
- 5 destroyers/frigates
- 2 landing ships logistic
- 2 Royal Fleet Auxiliaries
    (large supply ships)
- a varying number of merchant ships to provide accommodation and additional support, usually a further 8–10 large ships plus 5 smaller ships

RAF

- a squadron of Phantoms
- a squadron of Harriers
- Hercules aircraft
- Chinook helicopters
- Search & Rescue Sea King helicopters
- a squadron of Rapier air defence missile systems

Army

- a battalion of infantry (strengthened)
- 7 squadrons of engineers
- a logistic regiment (including a port squadron)
- a battery of Rapiers
- a field battery RA
- a helicopter squadron
- a signal squadron

During that intense and difficult first four months there were nail–biting moments most days and none more so than on the engineering side. To see 50–ton rock crushers being carried ashore by Mexeflote rafts in strong wind conditions, to be landed on basic slipways built out of necessity by Royal Engineers because no suitable jetties or cranes existed, was to call on the power of prayer; rock drills were working on rock which was found to be so hard it put the drills to exceptional strain – British industry responded at all hours of the day to get spares to us quickly. Meanwhile the maintenance of support (water, power, hygiene) facilities needed urgent daily attention, and the ever–present problem of the clearance of the debris of war, including booby–traps and munitions, called for unromantic courage and sweat unremittingly. Casualties occurred and set–backs were not infrequent. Elsewhere versatility was also the order of the day: the 1936 Bakery from the Aldershot Museum, set up in Stanley, was producing superb bread, and new laundry and shower arrangements were established. Meanwhile, live–firing ranges of high quality were creating unparalleled opportunities for realistic training for the infantry and the close support artillery, together with the Harriers and Naval Gunfire Support.

While this was going on, an important decision in principle was taken by the Ministry of Defence, on our initiative, to lease a floating hotel (called a Coastel) from a Swedish company. This would absolve the Royal Engineers from building an additional camp for 1,000 men near Stanley, and had the virtue that the Coastel could be redeployed elsewhere if force levels changed or if there was a decision to build the new airfield well away from Stanley. A further decision to build a radar station on the top of Mount Kent gave greater concern because of the intense logistic problems of building a major radar station on top of a mountain up which there was no access except by helicopter. But plans were laid accordingly.

The Falklands Intermediate Port and Storage System (FIPASS) opened on 31 March 1984. It provided storage facilities for the garrison's supplies which had previously to be kept on board ships anchored in the harbour. *Courtesy of Lieutenant-Colonel C M StG Kirke*

Now, with the airfield fully operational by mid–October, minefields better secured, and the basic facilities coming gradually under control, the next task was to build six camps and a major radar station before the onset of the next winter in May 1983. Throughout the next few months a remorseless drive was sustained to bring this accommodation into being on time. It is to the great credit of the Royal Engineers, and those who supplied them throughout the long chain back to the United Kingdom, that the major camp programme was completed by April 1983. Perhaps the finest engineering feat of all was to build the vital radar site on top of Mount Kent, sometimes in cloud, always wind–battered – and again on time. The plaque on that mountain reads: 'Zeus – a routine project for 34 Field Squadron'. Such was the spirit of that time.

It was also deeply satisfying to be able successfully to move the massive floating Coastel into its intricate and extensive moorings in the Canache inlet by the airfield in early January. The timing of this very difficult procedure was critical, relating to tides and very narrow margins of error both on water depths and widths of the vessel as set against the narrow neck of the Canache. The Prime Minister herself was aware during her inspiring visit to the Islands from 6 to 10 January, that unless we got the vessel into position by 12 January, we would have to wait a further three to four weeks for the next favourable tide, and 1,000 servicemen would yet again have been denied good accommodation. It was entirely fitting that this achievement should have come at the end of her visit.

While this race against time proceeded there was a sad duty to perform. It was necessary to collect all our own dead and, dependent on the wishes of the families concerned, either to bury them in a special cemetery at San Carlos, or to return them home to the United Kingdom. This grim and highly emotive business was concluded at the end of October 1982, and coincided with the visit of John Nott, Secretary of State for Defence. Soldiers of the Royal Pioneer Corps, under Major Robb, had to carry out this depressing task; they did it well. The Defence Secretary attended the ceremony of burial of the British servicemen at the permanent cemetery (chosen by those that fought the war). 14 bodies were buried there at a site that rests gently between the San Carlos Settlement Manager's house (Pat Short) and the Blue Beach landing point where 3 Commando Brigade had landed. Across the bay was the field hospital location of Ajax Bay, and out in San Carlos Water lay the grave of HMS *Ardent* (with HMS *Antelope* out in the Falkland Sound). It was an intensely moving but simple ceremony – the distant, then steadily deepening, sound of the formation of saluting helicopters as they moved in, east to west, across the cemetery, was one of many poignant moments. Farewell was also said in proper fashion to the 67 bodies on board HMS *Sir Bedivere*, lying out in the bay, which then sailed for home at the end of the ceremony to the receding sound of a piper's lament. A wreath was cast on the waters in memory of those who died at sea, whilst a salute was fired by HMS *Glasgow*. Six months later, in April 1983, the dependants were able to attend another service of consecration by the Bishop to the Forces, at the cemetery now encircled by a fine wall of Fox Bay granite and with impressive memorial stones. The Chief of the Defence Staff led the mourners.

It was also clear that whereas the plan for the proper burial of our own dead, and the memorials, was good, the problem of the many Argentine dead (some unburied in the hills, many loosely and poorly interred in mass graves in Stanley and elsewhere) had to be vigorously addressed. Our determination to get the issue of the proper Christian burial of the Argentine servicemen resolved had led to agreement to bury them in a mass cemetery in Goose Green. We gladly prepared the Argentine graves (dug by Royal Engineers and the Royal Hampshire Regiment), and held a formal service of consecration with full military honours in February, conducted by Monsignor Spraggon, the senior Roman Catholic priest in the Falkland Islands.

The important side–issue of conservation of wildlife had also demanded careful handling. The internationally influential conservation lobby was concerned about the disruption that both the war, and the presence of a sizeable military community after the war, might have on the unique wildlife of the area. Of particular concern was the constant movement of helicopters throughout the region,

and the need to have certain sizeable tracts of land set aside for live–firing training. Our plan was based on choosing training areas well away from the main bird colonies and by educating all servicemen, but particularly helicopter pilots, about the need to treat the wildlife with respect. We appointed the training Staff Officer (Major John Charteris) as Conservation Officer, and set up an active dialogue with the conservationists of note, such as Lord Buxton in the United Kingdom and Ian Strange in the West Falklands, to ensure that they were content with our approach. The press became aware of our concern and gave us some helpful support. Meanwhile the word about conservation was spread constantly, and some very good briefing maps were issued. Later on, in March 1983, we arranged with *Survival* (Anglia) to have an educational film produced. This was very much the initiative of Lord Buxton and his daughter Cindy. One wonders whether many other major organizations would have taken such trouble over the wildlife, but it was for us an important part of our overall

South Atlantic Medal 1982 with rosette; Commemorative Medal issued by the Borough of Stockton-on-Tees, Cleveland, for services in the Falklands campaign 1982. Awarded to Gunner Martin Hosie, 12th Air Defence Regiment, Royal Artillery. *National Army Museum 9106-13*

effort to preserve as much as possible of life as it had always been in the Falkland Islands.

Looking back ten years later, what perspective can be obtained? Firstly, there must be great satisfaction that within nine months – and prior to the onset of winter in 1983 – the tasks of construction and rehabilitation had effectively been achieved. At the same time a highly professional operational tri–service force had been established. This provided constant assurance to the Falkland Islanders, who were all too aware of an enemy over the horizon. These engineering tasks were of a variety and size not seen in the British Army since 1945. The support for these tasks over long lines of communication, especially all aspects of supply of materials and expertise, had made extensive demands on all three Services and the Merchant Marine. Every challenge had been met, often in harsh and unforgiving weather conditions. As time drew on the sense of achievement was tangible; it needed to be to allow the tempo of work seven days a week to proceed unabated.

Secondly, the operational tri–service structure was so integrated, if only to reduce overheads and cut out any unnecessary manpower, that rivalries which can and do flourish in easier circumstances, were thrust aside. A high level of mutual respect for each other's capabilities became natural to all, and there was enjoyment in friendly rivalry rather than tension leading to occasional counter–productive jockeying for position and status. High demands on limited resources of people, time, and money led to a healthy, practical acceptance of the best options being adopted for the greater good. Parochial interests were seldom, if ever, in evidence.

Last, the relationship between the Falkland Islanders and the constantly changing and much larger military and merchant marine population had been handled with sensitivity. It was remarkably good. John Ezard of *The Guardian*, after nearly three months on the Islands, remarked in an inimitable article: 'It has been a popular, hard–worked, and, for its age, almost unnaturally well–behaved force. When it completes its planned move out of real houses into portable cabins on windy hillsides, there will be regret as well as relief.' Those who had feared the garrison 'would impose an intolerable burden' on the Falklanders, and would 'destroy the traditional life of this rural community', had been proved emphatically wrong. This concerted effort to remain at one and in tune with the people (and the wildlife!), whilst carrying out this dynamic drive to rehabilitate and construct, required sustained effort by everyone at all levels. It succeeded remarkably where many prophets of doom had predicted failure.

The irrepressible spirit of that time was everywhere in evidence and was epitomized never more clearly than when eight of the 16 Haulamatic trucks held on the Falklands were sunk in the harbour in February 1983 as a Mexeflote overturned in high winds. These vehicles were critical to our success in camp construction because they transported crushed rock via ships to camp sites around the Islands. This was a tremendous blow, but there was no hesitation. All eight vehicles were recovered from the bottom of the harbour during the next two weeks by a team of Army and Royal Navy divers, tugs, RCT Port Squadron, and the LSL *Sir Geraint*. Meanwhile 16 more trucks were sent down from the UK, to arrive eight weeks later.

So ended the first, and critical, phase of the protected peace.

Ten Years On – The Literature of the Falklands War

Dr Linda Washington (National Army Museum)

The Falklands crisis lasted just over ten weeks. The land battle lasted under a month. Despite the comparative brevity of the campaign the conflict is the subject of an avalanche of literature, already rivalling the amount devoted to some aspects of the Second World War. The official papers documenting the preparations and conduct of the campaign will not be released for another twenty years, and even then more sensitive items are likely to be retained for another forty–five or even seventy years. Yet the Greenwood Press has judged that there are now sufficient books, articles and memoirs to warrant the publication of a full bibliography to mark the tenth anniversary of the year Britain went to war. 1992 is likely to see a further outpouring of historical analysis and memoirs, and this seems an appropriate time to examine the publications that have emerged so far. While a short review cannot be exhaustive, it is possible to investigate the pattern of the literature and highlight some of the better, and the not–so–good, publications that have so far appeared.

For any historian of the conflict the key sources will be accounts written by participants in the dramas of April, May and June 1982. At a senior level these have been rather slow to appear, partly due to restrictions on serving personnel as well as an understandable reticence about such recent, sensitive events. On the political front the arrival of the former Prime Minister Margaret Thatcher's memoirs is keenly anticipated for the fresh information they potentially contain. The Falkland Islands Governor, Sir Rex Hunt, has timed his own recollections to coincide with the anniversary, as has Sir John 'Sandy' Woodward.

Undoubtedly the best of the military memoirs to emerge so far is *No Picnic: 3 Commando Brigade in the South Atlantic, 1982* (London, Leo Cooper, 1982) by the Brigade Commander, Major–General Julian Thompson. As is only to be expected from an officer who is now a Visiting Senior Research Fellow at the Department of War Studies, King's College, University of London, this is an excellent blend of direct experience and military judgement matched by few of his contemporaries. Writing concisely and with great precision he gives a well–paced account of the land campaign and conveys to the reader some sense of the huge personal responsibility he carried in those weeks. At the other end of the publishing scale Major Ian Winfield converted his diary into a modest but entertaining paperback *The Posties Went to War* (Worcester, Square One, 1990). In amusing style he illustrates the daily work and worries of the Postal and Courier Service which kept every serviceman in touch with his relatives and friends at home.

Some of the most informative and exciting accounts of individual army units during the war are to be found in the numerous regimental and corps magazines. These range from scholarly articles on the practical problems faced by the Military Survey section of the Royal Engineers in producing enough maps for the campaign (apparently every British Army operation seems to take place just off the corner of any given map), to light–hearted anecdotes of the journey south and life at the front. They paint a vivid picture of the British Army at work and play, the earliest appearing whilst the campaign was still in progress, and will provide ample material for an army of military historians and sociologists into the next century. Written for their comrades and ex–servicemen the articles are often full of in–house humour, technical jargon, and abbreviations.

Some authors have tried to interpret the service stories for a more general readership and these publications are particularly valuable as they include many individuals who would not

Soldier photographer Paul Haley was the only official photographer on board *Queen Elizabeth II*. His pictures of life on board and of key events in the campaign appeared in national newspapers and on television. *Soldier: Magazine of the British Army*

otherwise publish their memories. In 1983 Geoffrey Underwood and Maritime Books produced *Our Falklands War: the Men of the Falklands War Tell Their Story* which gathered together short accounts by prominent figures, such as Commodore Michael Clapp and Commander Christopher Wreford–Brown, captain of HMS *Conqueror* which sank the *General Belgrano*. Three years later Max Arthur published a series of interviews with servicemen and women as *Above All, Courage: The Falklands Front Line* (London, Guild Publishing, 1985), covering a range of diverse experiences.

Many of the earliest serious studies of the whole crisis were written by news reporters,

either those accompanying the Task Force or those based in London and Washington. One 'instant' journalist's eye view was by Brian Hanrahan and Robert Fox, with the memorable title *I Counted Them All Out and I Counted Them All Back* (London, BBC, 1982), words used by Hanrahan to evade censorship when reassuring radio listeners of the safe return to HMS *Hermes* of the Harriers which had made the first attack on Stanley. The text consists mainly of short extracts from their radio and television broadcasts depicting life aboard ship and the fighting which followed. As well as the excitement of battle they accurately convey the intervening lulls and constant efforts to stay warm and comfortable, Robert Fox confessing that one of his greatest 'crises of communication' occured after Goose Green, 'wondering whether my brain could keep my big toe in contact long enough to stave off frost–bite'.

While Hanrahan and Fox adapted well to co–existence with the Services, Patrick Bishop of *The Observer* and John Witherow of *The Times* who wrote *The Winter War* (London, Quartet, 1982), found themselves in an alien world. Both travelled south with the Task Force on the *Invincible* and the *Canberra* and have no hesitation in describing a seamier, downbeat side to their experiences of life with the British Army, admitting that 'the military was a foreign country to most of us'. The days of National Service being long past, few of the journalists knew how the army operated and the character sketches here reflect the potential shipboard tensions. The next year Robert McGowan and Jeremy Hands let the other ranks speak for themselves, 'often profane, usually funny', in *Don't cry for me, Sergeant–Major* (London, Futura).

Other journalistic endeavours produced more conventional histories of widely varying quality. Christopher Dobson and Ronald Payne, together with John Miller of the *Daily Telegraph* – what the cover describes as 'a top investigative team' – produced *The Falklands*

Conflict (London, Coronet, 1982). None of the three were with the Task Force, and it shows. Claiming to be a 'full authoritative account', the result reads as an unexciting, rather pedestrian string of anecdotes instead of an in–depth analysis. Of 213 pages only 27 are devoted to the land campaign, some days reduced to only a paragraph of text. Avoiding yet another attempt to tell the 'whole' story, the *Sunday Express* team set out to fill a gap by documenting the war visually and produced *War in the Falklands: The Campaign in Pictures* (London, Weidenfeld and Nicolson, 1982), a selection of the best official and unofficial photographs which tried to remove some of the 'mystery' they felt still surrounded the campaign.

The best of the journalistic publications has become the popular standard history of the campaign, judging by sales figures, despite the fact that the passage of ten years means that some of its conclusions must be reassessed in the light of new evidence. Max Hastings had been a war reporter in the Middle East and Far East and had published studies of Bomber Command and Northern Ireland before joining the Task Force. His co–author, Simon Jenkins, was Political Editor of *The Economist* at the time of writing and covered the diplomatic background while Hastings concentrated on the fighting, becoming famous or notorious to his fellow 'hacks' as 'the first man into Stanley'. The authors wisely waited a while before going to press, giving time for further interviews with servicemen and diplomats, and at its publication *The Battle for the Falklands* (London, Michael Joseph, 1983) was full of fresh information, covering areas so far largely unexplained to the general public. It took the first real step in turning a remote, almost fantastic, war into hard, documented, fact, though the account of the action is necessarily laid on with a broad brush, containing little of the tactical or technical information that would emerge in later days. About to be republished, the book is still a very good recreation of the mood of the time.

Over the next few years, in the mid and late 1980s, came objective studies of the Falklands campaign written by authors who had no direct part in the campaign, either as participants or observers. Writer Martin Middlebrook deliberately waited until 1985 to allow 'the dust to settle' before producing *Operation Corporate: The Falklands War* (London, Viking, 1985) in which he concentrates on the military side of the crisis. It is based on his own interviews with servicemen and he has put together a more detailed account than Hastings, though it lacks some of the immediacy and drama. A more objective view emerges with distance, the soldiers admitting to occasionally low morale and pessimism. An excellent account for the popular reader, it is also a basic reference source for the more serious student of the campaign. Any collection of books on the war should also include that by Derek Oakley, an ex–Royal Marine, who produced a very well–illustrated, clear and succinct account of military and political events, and also broke new ground by looking at the individual contributions made by all branches of the services in essays examining their organization, tactics, weapons and vehicles. Middlebrook and Oakley should be supplemented by Gordon Smith's *Battles of the Falklands War* (London, Ian Allan, 1989). Half–way between a narrative and a chronology, it breaks the campaign down week by week, area by area, outlining the main progress with detailed maps and tables.

Other authors have found their particular sphere of interest in narrower aspects of the struggle to retake the Islands. Roger Perkins, a former soldier, mortgage and life assurance broker turned military and naval researcher, focussed on *Operation Paraquat: The Battle for South Georgia* (Bath, Picton Publishing, 1986). He goes into fine detail not to be found elsewhere on the history, geography and wildlife of an area home to one of the world's largest whaling stations, while his account of the campaign is a good blend of historical hindsight and dramatic incident. Descriptions of the weapons employed in the war tend to be confined to specialized text–books, but Bryan Perrett has brought all artillery pieces, small arms and armoured vehicles together in a useful little paperback *Weapons of the Falklands Conflict* (Poole, Blandford Press, 1982). While attributing the main credit for victory to the skill of the British troops using them, Perrett assesses the technical capability of each item as well as its actual performance in the war.

Outside the regimental and corps magazines and the press, only one writer has so far chosen to look at the long–term consequences of the war, both for the Falkland Islanders and the British forces stationed there. Major–General Edward Fursdon had previously served as Military Adviser to the Governor of Rhodesia in the period immediately prior to independence, and then as Senior British Officer in Zimbabwe before he retired in 1980 and joined the *Daily Telegraph* as its Defence and Military Correspondent. His six weeks in the South Atlantic during the summer of 1982 resulted in an unusual book *Falklands Aftermath: Picking Up the Pieces* (London, Leo Cooper, 1988) in which he investigates the impact of the war on the Islands' inhabitants, livestock and wildlife. With many entertaining tales Fursdon recounts

Argentine prisoners of war in sheep sheds in the Bluff Cove/Fitzroy area.
Express Newspapers/Airborne Forces Museum

his travels all over the area meeting the people, looking at the hazardous clear–up tasks such as mine disposal, the accommodation problems faced by the Army, the difficulties of raising families in the region, and the huge investment of finance and manpower needed to repair an estimated £35 million of war damage. The story is brought up to date as far as 1986 with the start of the new airfield project and the problem of over–fishing in Falkland waters.

The local inhabitants have also had their say in the historiography of the war. In 1984 John Smith, who had lived there since 1960, published *74 Days: An Islander's Diary of the Falklands Occupation* (London, Century). A member of the Falkland Islands Executive and Legislative Councils he provides an atmospheric account of listening to the local radio station's phone–in as Islanders described the invasion in progress, and the anxious hours waiting for the BBC to transmit news. Smith performs an invaluable service for early historians of the conflict by reproducing in full the edicts issued by the occupying power. *Faith Under Fire* (Basingstoke, Marshalls Paperbacks, 1983) by Harry Bagnall, the Anglican Chaplain on the Islands, was written as a retrospective memoir with the aid of a professional writer, rather than based on a contemporary diary, and lacks the power of Smith's work.

For a narrower readership there have been close scrutinies of the legalistic and ethical side of the conflict. The British Government's official viewpoint was published by HMSO in 1982 as *The Disputed Islands*, a short booklet which came out just after the crisis began. Declaring that 'Britain remains fully committed to the search for a diplomatic solution to the crisis which is obviously preferable to military confrontation' it nevertheless made it clear that the world ought to be in no doubt of British determination that the Falkland Islanders should maintain their way of life and decide their own allegiance. In the same year Yale University Press reprinted Julius Goebel's

1927 study of *The Struggle for the Falkland Islands: A Study in Legal and Diplomatic History*. A newly–added introduction by John Metford, Emeritus Professor of Spanish at the University of Bristol, pointed out that Goebel's decision in favour of the Argentine claim must be seen in the light of the sentiments of 1927, when colonialism was seen as the root cause of destructive European rivalries, though he had approached the problem with 'commendable scholarly integrity'.

More recently, professional historians have begun to place the crisis in some kind of socio–political context. Lawrence Freedman, Professor of War Studies at King's College, University of London, looked at the social impact of the war in *Britain and the Falklands War* (London, Basil Blackwell, 1988), part of the 'Making of Contemporary Britain' series aimed at undergraduates and sixth formers. The cover photograph proclaims his intention to examine the less palatable consequences of the British repossession of the Islands: two soldiers in wheelchairs, one of them having lost a leg, are seen in conversation with Margaret Thatcher. The text examines the subject impartially by presenting the Government's case point–by–point as a basis for discussion rather than prejudging it.

One of the most prominent trends in the literature has been to look at the 'lessons' learned from the war. Appropriately, the first word to the public on this subject came from Her Majesty's Government in December 1982 when the Secretary of State for Defence presented to Parliament *The Falklands Campaign: The Lessons* (London, HMSO). This brief, 46–page report concisely outlined Britain's reaction to the crisis with impressive matter–of–factness, and studied the implications for Britain's role in NATO, and for the future defence budget. In a conclusion to be echoed again and again in the popular literature the report decided that 'the basic ingredients for success were present ... a firm resolve;

flexibility of forces, equipment and tactics; human ingenuity; and well trained officers and men.' Elsewhere, the debate continued out of the public eye, partly in the service magazines and journals where the practical problems were identified and tackled.

Medicine has often progressed through lessons gained on the battlefield, but outside service medical journals this aspect of the Falklands campaign has understandably been largely ignored by authors because of its distressing nature. A very readable autobiographical account was given by Surgeon Commander Rick Jolly, in charge of the Royal Marines Medical Squadron. As the flyleaf of *The Red and Green Life Machine* (London, Corgi, 1983) points out, it was the first book about the campaign by a non–journalist. Though he has to depict in some harrowing detail the tragic result of bullets, shrapnel and helicopter crashes, Jolly concentrates on the positive response of his medical team, who carried on working despite two unexploded bombs in the building, and on their marvellous boast that 'everyone who reached Ajax Bay alive had gone out alive.' Simon Weston's and Robert Lawrence's stories reveal how they struggled to overcome the terrible injuries they suffered, Weston on the *Sir Galahad (Walking Tall* (London, Bloomsbury, 1989)), Lawrence on Mount Tumbledown *(When the Fighting is Over* (London, Bloomsbury, 1988)).

Reporters covering the campaign and publishing their own versions were soon to find themselves under scrutiny. The original stimulus was provided by Government criticism of the BBC for what it saw as biased broadcasting, and the retaliation by Fleet Street which defended journalistic independence and integrity. Robert Harris's *Gotcha!: The Media, The Government and the Falklands Crisis* (London, Faber and Faber, 1983) was titled after the famous *Sun* headline in the aftermath of the sinking of the Argentine battleship *General Belgrano* with heavy loss of life. For the first

The slow, measured tones of Ian MacDonald, the Ministry of Defence's acting Head of Public Relations, seen here with Lieutenant–Colonel Tim Donkin Royal Marines, became for many the voice of the Falklands War. *Frank Spooner*

time the book revealed the initially inadequate allocation made by the Ministry of Defence for journalists to accompany the Task Force – only five were scheduled to go before the Prime Minister's Press Secretary intervened. The author catalogues the technical and procedural difficulties encountered in bringing the story to the public; by the time the Task Force reached Ascension Island one senior MOD Public Relations Officer who had been trying to keep the peace between military and press was in such a state of nervous exhaustion that he was dispatched home. Technical hinderances, combined with what some saw as heavy–handed censorship, resulted in what one journalist described as 'the worst reported war since the Crimea'.

No survey of the Falklands literature would be complete without a brief glance at the enemy's viewpoint. Argentina's publications on the war tend to reiterate a profound belief in their country's right to sovereignty over the Falklands, though often criticising the junta's

conduct of the invasion and defence of the Islands. In Britain, Argentine opinion was first emotively stated in journalist Daniel Kon's work *Los Chicos de la Guerra* Sevenoaks, (New English Library, 1983). He had been inspired to write by the callous attitude displayed to returning Prisoners of War, and by a desire to learn more about the conflict. A series of interviews with young conscripts confirmed rumours of poor conditions and bad leadership, though many of his subjects obviously over–dramatized their accounts, particularly when describing encounters with the Gurkhas. A sober British account of the Argentine experience came years later with Martin Middlebrook's *The Fight for the 'Malvinas': The Argentine Forces in the Falklands War* (London, Viking, 1989). Refused entry to Argentina when he was writing his earlier account of the conflict, Middlebrook was eventually granted a visa in 1987 and found his 62 Argentine interviewees proud to have fought for the Islands, though admitting that they had often been misled by their officers and fed blatant lies in an effort to keep up their morale.

The conflict has also fascinated non–combatant nations, whose authors have been divided between viewing the fight as a ridiculous and unjustified clash between two militaristic countries with little to recommend either, or as a military and diplomatic case study. Both these points of view are to be found in the United States which initially took a neutral stance between the two warring countries, though later giving support to Britain. R. Elliot and M. Jeffrey made their standpoint clear in *Tempest in a Teapot: the Falkland Islands War* (San Bernadino, The Borgo Press, 1983) with a frontispiece showing a fortified teapot at sea, chapter titles like 'Reading the Tea Leaves' and the claim that the rest of the world had been puzzled by 'this bizarre little war' which should never have happened. In contrast, Nora Kinzer Stewart, a US Army sociologist, opted for the academic 'case study' approach in her *Mates and Muchachos: Unit Cohesion in the Falklands/Malvinas War* (London, Brassey's, 1991). Taking a evenly–balanced stand on the issue of sovereignty Stewart looks at both the British and Argentine Armies, comparing cohesion, morale, motivation and unit performance as influenced by each country's military traditions, society, and culture. Her conclusion that 'the strength of the British forces was neither weapons nor technology but its men' is a common theme throughout the literature on the Falklands war. At the other end of the political spectrum, the USSR's Academy of Sciences found little to support Britain's case in its work *The Malvinas/Falkland crisis: the causes and consequences* (Moscow, 1984). The Germans and French have confessed themselves equally bemused by a war at the other side of the world in which neither was asked to do more than put moral and economic pressure on Argentina.

Despite the tragedy and pathos that are so evident in the factual accounts, the Falklands conflict has not been the subject of a great deal of fiction; amateur authors seemingly still prefer the 'glamourous' red coats of the nineteenth century to the gritty modern reality that is so hard to portray convincingly. But the campaign has earned its place in the history of art. Linda Kitson's sketches combine the urgency of technological warfare with moving depictions of the men behind the guns and were immediately published as *The Falklands War: A Visual Diary* (London, Mitchell Beazley/Imperial War Museum, 1982). The Manchester City Art Gallery incorporated many other viewpoints in its exhibition on *The Falklands Factor: Representations of a Conflict*, published in 1989, looking at how the war 'has affected the consciousness of the people of this country as a whole and how this has been described or expressed through visual means'. The works included range from collages produced by veterans during post–traumatic stress therapy at the Royal Naval Psychiatric Hospital, to cynical caricatures by the cartoonist Ralph Steadman in the *New Statesman*.

If the literature surrounding the invasion and recovery of the Falklands reflects any clear pattern, it is the manifold reasons behind the enduring attraction many authors feel towards the conflict. Essentially, it was a war that the British took very personally; despite the need to enlist the moral support of the United Nations and British success in winning some practical aid from the United States, only Britain and Argentina faced each other on the field of battle. The recent Gulf conflict involved many coalition nations and may not have gripped the emotions of the British public in quite the same way. Everyone over 20 years old who listened to the radio or watched television at the time still remembers the news flashes, the slow, measured tones of the Ministry of Defence spokesman, the crowds outside Downing Street, and the sight of wounded servicemen coming ashore from the *Sir Galahad*. On top of this, the war was, to begin with, hidden from public view, despite the presence of dozens of military pundits on television news and current affairs programmes. Reporting restrictions and the 8,000 mile distance meant that the rest of the world only saw pictures of events days or even weeks after they had taken place; many authors felt the need to compensate for this and by the time the first elements of the Task Force returned home 'instant' histories were already coming off the presses.

The sheer quantity of publications also indicates the rapid multiplication of the number of professional and amateur authors over the past ten years. The word–processing revolution means that, for a relatively modest cost, retired insurance salesmen, ex–servicemen and hundreds of others can analyse and re–evaluate the campaign to satisfy a professional and public curiosity which has still not faded. But perhaps the greatest reason for the fascination with the Falklands War is precisely its brevity and comprehensiveness. Compressed into ten tense weeks was a protracted diplomatic drama, a sea battle on a scale not seen for nearly 40 years, an air war using the very latest technology, culminating in a hand–to–hand confrontation. Units and individuals can be followed day by day, their decisions and tactics explored in a detail not possible ten years after the Second World War. Publications of every type explored above will continue to appear side by side in the bookshops for many years; the new phase of writing will not commence until the first release of Prime Ministerial, War Cabinet, Foreign Office and Ministry of Defence papers in 2013. Then the revelations will begin.

The British military cemetery at San Carlos soon after the war. *Airborne Forces Museum*

Further Reading

Adams, V *The Media and the Falklands Campaign* London, Macmillan, 1986

Barnett, A *Iron Britannia* London, Allison and Busby, 1982

Battle for the Falklands (3 vols) London, Osprey, 1982

Carr, R *Up the Falklands: Cartoons from the Royal Marines* Poole, Blandford Press, 1982

Cobb, D *The Falklands Paintings* London, Conway Maritime Press, 1986

The Covenanter 1/7th Gurkhas, 1982, No 16, pp 27–29

The Craftsman REME, December 1982, Vol 38, No 12, pp 340–356

Dabat, A and Lorenzano, L *Argentina, the Malvinas and the end of Military Rule* London, Verso Editions, 1984

Dar, E H 'Problems of land strategy in the Falklands War', in *Pakistan Army Journal*, December 1982, Vol 23, No 4, pp 26–34

Daynes, J A *The Forces Postal History of the Falkland Islands and the Task Force* Forces Postal History Society, 1983

'The Falklands; an account of 4th Field Regiment activities' in *The Gunner*, August 1982, No 141, pp 17–20

'Falkland Islands' in *The Royal Pioneer*, December 1982, Vol 36, No 152, pp 29–32

'The Falkland Islands Campaign' in *Army Medical Services Magazine*, October 1982, Vol 26, pp 58 & 85–87

Falklands Task Force Portfolio (2 vols) Liskeard, Maritime Books, 1983

The Falklands War: the official history London, Latin American Newletters, 1983

Fox, R *Eyewitness Falklands* London, Methuen, 1982

Frost, J *2 Para Falklands: The Battalion at War* London, Buchan and Enright, 1983

The Guards Magazine Summer 1982, entire issue

Journal of the Royal Army Chaplains' Department December 1982, Vol 27, No 2, pp 18–21

Gamba, V *The Falklands/Malvinas War: A Model for North–South Crisis Prevention* Boston, Allen and Unwin, 1982

Laffin, J *Fight for the Falklands* London, Sphere Books, 1982

'New Light on electronic warfare in the Falklands campaign' in *Defence Today*, April 1983, Issue 60, p 124

Naafi News, July–August 1982, No 202, pp 6–11

Pegasus Parachute Regiment, July 1982, Vol 37, No 3, pp 4–8

Pochhacker, C 'Roland and Milan in the Falklands' in *Defence Update International*, 1985, No 61, pp 63–65

RAOC Gazette, September 1982, Vol 64, No 4, p 141

The Rose and Laurel, December 1982, Vol 10, No 5, pp 34–35

Rose, H M 'Towards an Ending of the Falklands War, June 1982' in *Conflict*, 1987, Vol 7, No 1, pp 1–13

Royal Corps of Transport Review, 1983, Vol 2, No 15

Royal Military Police Journal, 1982, Vol 33, No 1, p 46

The Sapper Royal Engineers, August 1982, Vol 20, No 10, pp 390–397

Soldier: Magazine of the British Army, Vol 38, Nos 17, 19, 22; Vol 39, No 2

Spicer, T S 'Return to the Falkland Islands' in *The Guards Magazine*, Spring 1983, pp 14–17

The Sunday Times Insight Team *The Falklands War* London, Andre Deutsch, 1982

'The Task Force Triumphed' in *The Wire*, July 1982, Vol 36, No 4, p 257

Turolo, C M *Malvinas: Testimonio de su Gobernador* Buenos Aires, Sudamericana, 1983

Tustin, W J 'The Logistics of the Falklands War' in *The Army Quarterly*, July 1984, Vol 114, No 3, p 301

Vaux, N *March to the South Atlantic* London, Buchan and Enright, 1986

Watson, B W and Dunn, P M eds *Military Lessons of the Falkland Islands War: Views from the United States* London, Arms and Armour Press, 1984

Lieutenant–Colonel Herbert 'H' Jones, Commanding Officer of 2 Para, who was killed in action at Goose Green and awarded a posthumous VC. *Airborne Forces Museum*

Victoria Cross 1982; The Most Excellent Order of The British Empire (OBE) 1981; General Service Medal 1962, with clasp: Northern Ireland; South Atlantic Medal 1982 with rosette; Elizabeth II Silver Jubilee Medal 1977. Awarded to Lieutenant–Colonel Herbert Jones, 2nd Battalion, The Parachute Regiment. *Loan: Mrs S Jones 8311–32*

Corporal Brian Washington, 3 Para, seen here talking to the Colonel-in-Chief, HRH The Prince of Wales, on Airborne Forces Day, 1978, enlisted into the Regiment in 1956 and is the only member of 3 Para to have served both at Suez and in the Falklands. *National Army Museum 9201–14*

General Service Medal (Army and RAF) 1918–62 with clasp: Near East; General Service Medal 1962 with clasps: Radfan, Northern Ireland; United Nations Medal for Cyprus; South Atlantic Medal 1982 with rosette; Army Long Service and Good Conduct Medal 1977. Awarded to Corporal B N Washington, 3rd Battalion, The Parachute Regiment. *National Army Museum 9112–133*

Colour Sergeant Brian Faulkner, 3 Para, who was awarded the Distinguished Conduct Medal for his part in the capture of Mount Longdon. *National Army Museum 9001–23*

Distinguished Conduct Medal 1982; General Service Medal 1962 with clasp: Northern Ireland; United Nations Medal for Cyprus; South Atlantic Medal 1982 with rosette; Army Long Service and Good Conduct Medal. Awarded to Warrant Officer II Brian Faulkner, 3rd Battalion, The Parachute Regiment. *National Army Museum 8912–62*

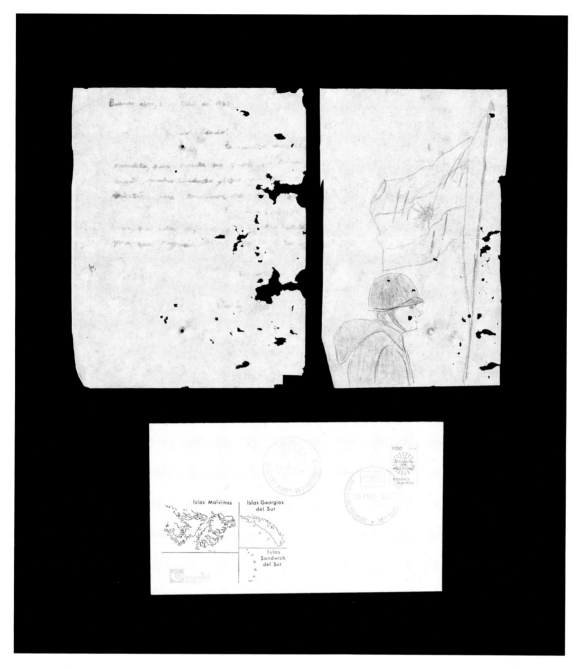

Contact with home was an important element in the morale of both sides in the conflict.

Top: letter and drawing sent by a school child to an Argentine conscript. They were recovered from a trench near Mount Tumbledown in early July.

Bottom: a philatelic cover sent from the 'Islas Malvinas' to Buenos Aires, 29 May 1982.

National Army Museum 9006–150

A registered first day cover sent from Adelaide Island to England. In transit the letter passed through Port Stanley just as the Argentines invaded and was finally dispatched on 6 April with the date-stamp '9409 Islas Malvinas * Republica Argentina', in addition to the original British Antarctic Territory transit stamp.

National Army Museum 9006-150

Chronology

1982

19 March Argentine scrap metal merchants land on South Georgia

2 April Argentine invasion of the Falklands

British Task Force prepared

3 April Royal Marines on South Georgia overwhelmed

UN passes Resolution 502 demanding immediate Argentine withdrawal

Emergency meeting of Parliament

5 April Task Force sails from Portsmouth

Lord Carrington resigns

7 April US peace mission launched

9 April *Canberra* leaves Portsmouth with 3 Para, 40, and 42 Commandos

12 April Maritime Exclusion Zone declared around the Falklands

17 April Admiral Fieldhouse, C–in–C Fleet, holds briefing on Ascension Island for British commanders

21 April SAS and SBS land on South Georgia

26 April Argentine forces on South Georgia surrender

30 April President Reagan declares US support for Britain

1 May SAS and SBS land on the Falklands

British bombing raids on Stanley and Goose Green airfields

2 May *General Belgrano* sunk

Peace proposals tabled by both UN and Peru

4 May HMS *Sheffield* sunk

7 May Amphibious Task Group leaves Ascension Island

Peruvian peace plan withdrawn

12 May *QEII* leaves Southampton with 5 Infantry Brigade

14 May SAS destroys Argentine aircraft on Pebble Island

18 May UN–mediated peace process ends

19 May	War Cabinet approves plan for San Carlos landings	*2 June*	2 Para helicopters forward to Bluff Cove
	Helicopter cross–decking accident leaves 18 SAS men dead	*4 June*	Britain and US veto cease–fire resolution at UN
21 May	San Carlos landings	*6 June*	2nd Scots Guards lands at Fitzroy
25 May	HMS *Coventry* and *Atlantic Conveyor* sunk	*8 June*	*Sir Galahad* and *Sir Tristram* bombed at Fitzroy: 51 dead, mostly Welsh Guardsmen
26 May	2 Para marches on Goose Green		Orders Group on HMS *Fearless* finalises plan for attack Port Stanley
27 May	3 Para and 45 Commando begin march to Teal Inlet		
	SAS land on Mount Kent	*11 June*	Battle for Port Stanley begins: attack by 3 Para on Mount Longdon; by 42 Commando on Mount Harriet; by 45 Commando on Two Sisters
28 May	Battle at Goose Green		
	5 Infantry Brigade completes cross–decking at South Georgia	*12 June*	Objectives taken
29 May	Argentines surrender at Goose Green	*13 June*	Attack by 2 Para on Wireless Ridge; by 2nd Scots Guards on Mount Tumbledown; by 1/7th Gurkha Rifles on Mount William
30 May	General Moore arrives in the Falklands		
	42 Commando begins flying forward to Mount Kent	*14 June*	Argentines on the Falklands surrender
31 May	Argentine special forces routed at Top Malo House		
1 June	5 Infantry Brigade begins disembarkation at San Carlos		

British Land Forces Order of Battle

3 Commando Brigade

Brigade Headquarters

29 Commando Regiment Royal Artillery

59 Independent Commando Squadron Royal Engineers

40 Commando Royal Marines

42 Commando Royal Marines

45 Commando Royal Marines

2, 3, and 6 Sections Special Boat Squadron

Mountain and Arctic Warfare Cadre Royal Marines

3 Commando Brigade Air Squadron Royal Marines

605, 611, and 612 Tactical Air Control Parties Royal Marines

3 Commando Brigade Headquarters and Signals Squadron Royal Marines, including Number 1 Raiding Squadron and Air Defence Troop

Y Signals Troop Royal Marines

Commando Logistic Regiment Royal Marines

Commando Forces Band Royal Marines (plus Surgical Support Teams)

plus attached units:

Two Troops of B Squadron, RHG/D The Blues and Royals

Forward Observation Officers of 4 Field Regiment Royal Artillery

T Battery, 12 Air Defence Regiment Royal Artillery

Detachment 49 Explosive Ordnance Disposal Squadron, 33 Engineer Regiment (plus EOD Team, Royal Air Force)

Element Postal and Courier Regiment Royal Engineers

Rear Link Detachment 30 Signal Regiment Royal Signals

613 Tactical Air Control Party

2nd Battalion The Parachute Regiment, with attached units:–

29 Battery, 4 Field Regiment Royal Artillery;
Troop from 43 Air Defence Battery;
32 Guided Weapons Regiment Royal Artillery;
Troop from 9 Parachute Engineer Squadron;
Troop from 16 Field Ambulance Royal Army Medical Corps

3rd Battalion The Parachute Regiment

D and G Squadrons 22nd Special Air Service Regiment

One Flight 656 Squadron Army Air Corps

Detachments 47 Air Despatch Squadron and 17 Port Regiment Royal Corps of Transport

Detachment 81 Ordnance Company Royal Army Ordnance Corps

5 Infantry Brigade

Brigade Headquarters

Headquarters and 97 Battery, 4 Field Regiment Royal Artillery

One troop of 43 Air Defence Battery, 32 Guided Weapons Regiment Royal Artillery

36 Engineer Regiment Royal Engineers

9 Parachute Squadron Royal Engineers

Brigade Headquarters and Signal Squadron with Rear Link Detachments Royal Signals

2nd Battalion Scots Guards

1st Battalion Welsh Guards

1st Battalion 7th Duke of Edinburgh's Own Gurkha Rifles

Number 656 Squadron Army Air Corps

407 Road Transport Troop Royal Corps of Transport

16 Field Ambulance Royal Army Medical Corps

81 and 91 Ordnance Companies and 421 Explosive Ordnance Disposal Company Royal Army Ordnance Corps

10 Field Workshop Royal Electrical and Mechanical Engineers

Elements 160 Provost Company Royal Military Police

8 Field Cash Office Royal Army Pay Corps

Medium and heavy–lift Helicopter availability for land operations from 21 May to 14 June 1982

compiled by Major–General Julian Thompson

From 21 May

11 Sea King Mk 4
5 Wessex Mk 5

but one Sea King remained embarked in *Canberra* when she sailed night 21/22 May. This helicopter never returned for land force tasks.

4 Sea Kings fitted with passive night goggle equipment for night use. Not available in daytime because of crew rest and maintenance for night operations. Not available for day use except in emergency.

1 Sea King dedicated to Rapier maintenance nearly all day initially.

Therefore daily availability actually:

5 Sea King Mk 4
5 Wessex Mk 5

26 May - 1 June

6 Sea King Mk 4	remaining Sea King allocated as above
5 Wessex Mk 5	
1 Chinook	without spares, or maintnance manuals or tools

From 1 June - 9 June

6 Sea King Mk 4	remaining Sea King allocated as above
19 Wessex Mk 5	
4 Sea King Mk 2	anti-submarine helicopters, with crews untrained in land operations
1 Chinook	without spares, maintenance manuals or tools

From 9 June - 14 June

6 Sea King Mk 4		Unserviceability starts to take effect
23 Wessex Mk 5		
10 Sea King Mk 2	(see comment above)	
1 Chinook	(see comment above)	

As an example of the demands on helicopter lift, it takes 82 Sea King sorties to lift a light gun battery with ammunition. The time this operation will take depends on the distance over which the battery has to be lifted. To restock a battery of guns with 480 rounds per gun takes 60 Sea King sorties, or 120 Wessex sorties, or 20 Chinook sorties. 3 Commando Brigade landed with three gun batteries, and two more came with 5 Infantry Brigade.

Glossary

Bandwagon	See BV202
Battery	The smallest self–contained sub–unit of artillery, normally of six or eight guns in two equal troops. Heavy and Medium batteries usually have fewer guns.
Blowpipe	Hand–held, wire–guided missile.
BV202	Tracked, articulated, over–snow towing vehicle and trailer, built by Volvo (Bandwagon)
cct	Circuit
CDS	Chief of the Defence Staff
CGS	Chief of the General Staff
C–in–C	Commander–in–Chief
CVRT	Combat Vehicle Reconnais-sance Tracked – Scimitar or Scorpion light tank
C–130	Argentine four–engined, short take–off and landing transport aircraft
DF	Defensive Fire – pre–recorded and adjusted artillery, mortar or machine gun fire by troops in defensive positions against attacking troops or patrols
DFC	Distinguished Flying Cross
EFI	Expeditionary Force Institutes
FAC	Forward Air Controller
FAL	Argentine rifle that fires automatic or single rounds
FIBS	Falkland Islands Broadcasting Service
FOO	Forward Observation Officer – an artillery officer provided from the battery supporting the battalion or Commando
FUP	Forming Up Position – the area behind the Start Line (qv) in which assaulting troops form up for an assault
GPMG	General Purpose Machine Gun – belt–fed 7.62mm weapon, normally one per section in every British battalion or Commando
GPMG (SF)	Mounted on a tripod and equipped with a heavier barrel and dial sight to enable it to fire at night, or through smoke or mist, and hit pre–recorded targets. The kit to carry out the conversion is known as the Sustained Fire (SF) kit.
HE	High Explosive
HF	High Frequency
H–Hour	The time at which the first wave of assaulting troops cross the Start Line (qv)
LCU	Landing Craft Utility – landing craft capable of carrying 200 men, or 22 tons of stores, or four large trucks
LSL	Landing Ship Logistic – roll–on–roll–off ships designed to carry tanks, trucks and logistic supplies for an amphibious operation.

Milan	Wire–guided, anti–tank missile, useful for bunker–busting	**RHG/D**	Royal Horse Guards/1st Dragoons – The Blues and Royals
MOD PR	Ministry of Defence Public Relations	**RM**	Royal Marines
NAAFI	Navy, Army and Air Force Institutes	**RMP**	Royal Military Police
NATO	North Atlantic Treaty Organization	**SACC**	Supporting Arms Co–ordination Centre
NBC	Nuclear, Biological, Chemical warfare	**Sangar**	A protective wall built of stone or peat–blocks by troops on ground too hard to dig trenches
NCO	Non–Commissioned Officer – soldier or marine holding a rank between that of private and Warrant Officer	**SAS**	Special Air Service
		SBS	Special Boat Squadron
NGS	Naval Gunfire Support	**Scimitar**	Alvis–built light tank equipped with 30mm automatic cannon
NGSFO	Naval Gunfire Support Forward Observer	**Scorpion**	Alvis–built light tank equipped with 76mm gun and night–vision equipment
OP	Observation Post – a small, well–concealed position from which to observe	**Sixty–Six**	66mm – a shoulder–held light anti–armour weapon (LAW), anti–tank rocket in a throw–away launcher
Rapier	British–built surface–to–air missile mounted on quad launchers	**SLR**	Self–Loading Rifle
RAP	Regimental Aid Post	**SQMS**	Staff Quartermaster–Sergeant
RSM	Regimental Sergeant–Major	**Start Line**	A line on the ground, usually a natural feature, stream, bank or fence which marks the start line for an attack and is crossed at H–Hour (qv) in attack formation
RAMC	Royal Army Medical Corps		
RAOC	Royal Army Ordnance Corps		
RAPC	Royal Army Pay Corps		
RA	Royal Artillery	**STUFT**	Ships Taken Up From Trade – merchant ships requisitioned for war service
RCT	Royal Corps of Transport		
REME	Royal Electrical and Mechanical Engineers	**TEZ**	Total Exclusion Zone
		UHF	Ultra High Frequency
RE	Royal Engineers	**UN**	United Nations
RFA	Royal Fleet Auxiliary – the logistic ships for the Royal Navy, mainly storeships and oilers, but also LSLs (qv)	**VC**	Victoria Cross
		VHF	Very High Frequency

INDEX

Illustrations are indexed in italics

Adelaide Island, *102*
Ajax Bay, 23, 63, 69, 73, 76-7, 78, 80, 86
Aldershot, 85
Archer, Peter, *56, 61*
Argentina, 81, 83, 93, 94, 95
Argentine Air Force, 5, 11, 15, 21-3, 43, 51, *57, 59,* 72, 76-7
Argentine Land Forces, 46, 56, 57, 58, 59, 60, 63, 64, 65, *71, 72, 73,* 80, *92,* 94-5, *101*
    3rd Infantry Regiment, 38
    4th Infantry Regiment, 31, 36
    6th Infantry Regiment, 31-3, 36-7
    7th Infantry Regiment, 31, 38-9
    12th Infantry Regiment, 36
    Marine Engineers, 36-7
    5th Marines, 35-7
    602 Commando Company, 28
Argentine Navy, 7, 12, 16, 57
Argentine Special Forces, 59, *59*
Arthur, Max, 90
Ascension Island, 6, 7, 9, 12, 13, 25, 42, 43, 55, 56, 62, 63, 64, 66, 76, 94

Bagnall, Harry, 92
Ball, Anthony, 69
Barley, A K, 70
Bates, Peter, *52*
Bethell, Richard, 36
Bickerdike, Andrew, 32
Bishop, Patrick, 90
Bluff Cove, 17, 29, 63, 66, 70, 72, *92*
Boca House, 25
Boswell, Rod, 28
Bramall, Edwin, Lord Bramall, 5-18
British Antarctic Territory, *102*
British Land Forces,
    3 Commando Brigade, 13-39 *passim*, 41-8, 49, 51, 55, 59, 64, 71, 76, 77-8, 86; 5 Infantry Brigade, *11,* 14, 15, 17, 23, 27, 28-30, 35-9, 41-8, *42, 44,* 49, 51, 67, 69, 70, 71, 73, 77-8, *77, 79*
    Army:
        Blues and Royals, 20, 40, 41-8; Royal Artillery, 19, 30, 40, 43, 44, 49-54, *50, 52,* 60, 85, *87*; Royal Engineers, 19, 40, 44, 61-3, 78, *82,* 83, 84, 85, 86, 87, 89; Royal Signals, 40, 52, *56, 61,* 63-4, 85; 2nd Battalion Scots Guards, 14, 17, 26, 28, 29, 36-7, 39, 41, 42, *42,* 53, *55,* 62, 64; 1st Battalion Welsh Guards, 14, 15, 17, 18, 28-31, *30,* 42, *61,* 72, 78; Royal Hampshire Regiment, 87; 2nd Battalion Parachute Regi-
ment, 16-19, *20, 24,* 25-30, 35, 37-9, *38,* 41-8, *50,* 51, 60, 62, 64, 71, 77; 3rd Battalion Parachute Regiment, 17, 19, *21,* 25, 26, 27, *27,* 30-2, *32,* 37, 39, 41-8, *65, 68,* 72, 73; 1st/7th Gurkhas, 14, 17-18, 28, 39, 41, *41,* 42, *48,* 62, 64, 94; 22nd Special Air Service Regiment, 10, 13, 27, 28, 43, 52, 55-60, *55, 59, 60*; Army Air Corps, 40, 47-8, 64-5, 70; Royal Army Chaplains' Department, 65-6; Royal Corps of Transport, 66-8, 84, 87; Royal Army Medical Corps/Army Medical Services, 23, 47-8, 68-9; Royal Army Ordnance Corps, 76-80; Royal Electrical and Mechanical Engineers, 52, 69-70; Royal Military Police, 70-1, *71*; Royal Army Pay Corps, 52, 71-2; Royal Army Dental Corps, 69; Royal Pioneer Corps, 86 Intelligence Corps, 72-3; Army Catering Corps, 52, 73-4, *73*; Queen Alexandra's Royal Army Nursing Corps, 69
    Royal Marines, *7-8,* 8, 10, *13,* 15, 57, 60, 70, 71, 76, 93, 94
        40 Commando, 19, 27, 28-9, 30, 41, 46; 42 Commando, 17, 19, 26-8, 30, 31, 34-5, *35,* 39, 41, 46, 59, *59*; 45 Commando, 17, 18, 19, 25, 27, 30-4, *34,* 39, 41, 46; Special Boat Squadron, 13, 25, 44

Brize Norton, 67
Brownson, Derek, 84
Buxton, Aubrey, Lord Buxton, 87
Buxton, Cindy, 87

Camilla Creek House, 25, 64
Canache Inlet, 86
Charteris, John, 87
Chaundler, David, 37-8
Choiseul Sound, 29
Churchill, Sir Winston, 18
Clapp, Michael, 19, 22, 29, 90
Cooper, David, 66
Crosland, John, 25, 27

Dalzel-Job, Iain, 37
Darwin, 21, *24,* 25, 40, 43, 51, 58, 59, 64, 73
Dimmick, A E, 66
Dobson, Christopher, 90
Donkin, Tim, *94*
Douglas, 25, 45
Dytor, Clive, 33

Egg Harbour House, 64
Elliot, R, 95

Estancia House, 30, 45, *47*, 51, 59, 78
Ezard, John, 88

Falkland Islands Company, 80
Fanning Head, 23
Faulkner, Brian, *100*
Fieldhouse, Sir John, Lord Fieldhouse, 7-8, 10, 13-15, 25
Fitzroy, 20, 27, 29-30, *30*, 35, 36, 49, 62, 64, 70, 72, 73, 78, 80, *80*, *92*
Fortuna Glacier, 57
Fox, Robert, 63, 90
Fox Bay, 58, 59, 80, 82, 87
Freedman, Lawrence, 93
Fursdon, Edward, 92

Galtieri, Leopoldo, 12
Gibraltar, 6, 7
Goat Ridge, 34, 35, 36, 62
Goebels, Julius, 92
Goose Green, 15-17, 21, *24*, 25-7, *28*, 28, 30, 37, 40, 43, 46, 47, 51, 58, 59, 62, 64, 77, 82, 87, 90
Grass Island, 57
Green Patch, 45
Grytviken, 11, 57, *79*
Gurung, Ombhakta, *48*

Haig, Alexander, 6, 12
Haley, Paul, *90*
Hands, Jeremy, 90
Hanrahan, Brian, 90
Harris, Robert, 93
Hastings, Max, 91
Heardon Water, 60
Hosie, Martin, *87*
Howes, Philip, *84*
Hunt, Malcolm, 28
Hunt, Rex, 83, 89
Hussey, Barry Melbourne, 60

Iles, A, *62*

Jackson, Robert, 37
Jeffrey, M, 95
Jenkins, Simon, 91
Jolly, Rick, 93
Jones, Herbert, 16, 25, 26, 47, *98*

Keeble, Christopher, 25, 26, 29
Kirke, Charles, *6*, *86*
Kiszely, John, 37

Kitson, Linda, 95

Langham, David, 7
Lawrence, Robert, 93
Leach, Sir Henry, 5-16
Leith, 11, 57
Lewin, Terence, Lord Lewin, 6-16
Lively Island, 29
Lowe, Michael, 73
Lyneham, 67

MacDonald, Ian, *94*
McFaddyen, Ian, 84
McHale, M J, 69
McGowan, Robert, 90
McKay, Ian, 32
Mather, Gordon, *56*
Menendez, Mario, 54, 58, 59, 60
Merchant Navy, 81, 88
Metford, John, 92
Middlebrook, Martin, 91, 94
Miller, John, 90
Milne, J, 63
Moody Brook, 7, 30, 38
Montgomery, Robert, *18*
Moore, Sir Jeremy, 8, 13, 16, 17, 23, 25, 28, 30, *39*, 41, 49, 72
Mount Challenger, 28, 58
Mount Estancia, 28
Mount Harriet, *6*, 17, 29-31, 34-5, *35*, 36, 46, 47, 51, 70
Mount Kent, 23, 26-8, 30, 59, *59*, 70, 78, 85, 86
Mount Longdon, 17, 29-32, *32*, 37, 39, 44, 46, 47, 48, 51, *65*, 72
Mount Low, 59, 60
Mount Tumbledown, 17, 29-30, 33-7, *36*, 39, 41, 46, 47, 48, 53, 60, 62, 64, 81, 93, *101*
Mount Usborne, 20
Mount Vernet, 28
Mount William, 17-18, 29, 30, 35-6, 39, 62, 64
Murrell Heights, 59, 60
Murrell River/Bridge, 31, 32, 62

Naya, P H R, 69
Neame, Philip, 25, 38
Newland, Steven, 34
Niblett, Jeffrey, 64
Northwood, 7, 8, 14, 25, 27, 28, 29, 49, 72
Nott, John, 86
Nuemayer Glacier, 57

Oakley, Derek, 91

Payne, Ronald, 90
Pebble Island, 13, *57*, 58
Peck, Terry, 45
Pennicott, Brian, 49-54
Percival, Alan, 63
Perkins, Roger, 91
Perrett, Bryan, 92
Peru, 12
Pike, Hew, 25, 31-2, 40-48
Port Howard, 58, 82
Port Purvis, 58
Port Salvador, 23
Port San Carlos, 23, 27, 43, 45, 77, 82
Port Stanley, *8*, 9, 11, 14-30 *passim*, 35, 36, 37, 39, 40, 43, 45, *47*, 51, *54*, *56*, 58, 59, 60, 63, 67, 70, *71*, 72, 80, 81-2, *82*, 83, 84, *84*, 85, 90, 91, *102*
Price, Simon, 37

Quinn, Harold, 71

Reagan, Ronald, 12
Reffell, Derek, 85
Robb, John, 86
Roose, Seth, 62
Rose, Michael, 55-60, *57*, *59*, *60*
Royal Air Force, 7, 9, 46, 50, 62, 67, 71, 84

Royal Air Force Regiment, 49
Royal Fleet Auxiliary, 66, 85
    see also ships
Royal Navy, 6, 8, 10, 15, 40, 51, 57, 58, 62, 71, 85, 88
    see also ships
Royal Signals and Radar Establishment, 50

San Carlos, 8, 13, 15, 19, *21*, *22*, 21-3, 25, 28, 29, 40, 41, 43, 44, *44*, 49, 50, 51, *52*, *53*, 62, 63, 65, 66, 68, 69, 70, 71-2, 73, 77, *79*, 81, 83-4, 86, *96*
San Carlos Water, 58, 59, *61*, 76, 80
Sapper Hill, 18, 35, 36, 39, *54*
Scott, Michael, 36-7
Seal Point, 60
Sennybridge, 45
Ships: *Antelope*, 62, 77, 87; *Antrim*, 10, 57; *Ardent*, 87; *Atlantic Conveyor*, 15, 23, 25; *Baltic Ferry*, 77; *Canberra*, 15, 42, 68, 70, *79*, 90; *Cardiff*, 29; *Elk*, 76; *Endurance*, 57; *Europic Ferry*, 50; *Exeter*, 70; *Fearless*, 15, 23, 29, 53, 56, 67; *Fort Austin*, 55; *General Belgrano*, 11-12, 16, 93; *Glamorgan*, 58; *Glasgow*, 87; *Hermes*, *13*, 58, 90; *Intrepid*, 15, 29; *Invincible*, 90; *Norland*, *20*, 71; *Queen Elizabeth II*, *11*, 14, 25, *41*, 69, 70, 73, 77, *79*, 90; *Rangatira*, 81; *St Edmund*, 77; *Santa Fé*, 11; *Sheffield*, 11, 12; *Sir Bedivere*, 87; *Sir Galahad*, 15, 17, 29, *30*, 49, 66, 68, 76, 77, 78, *80*, 93, 95; *Sir Geraint*, 88;

Sir Lancelot, 76, 77; *Sir Percival*, 76; *Sir Tristram*, 29, *68*, 78, *80*; *Stromness*, 76
Short, Pat, 86
Smith, Gordon, 91
Smith, John, 92
Southampton, *11*, *50*, 70
Southby-Tailyour, Ewen, 29
South Cerney, 67
South Georgia, *4*, 7, 10-11, 12, 15, 26, 55, 56, 57, 58, *60*, 63, 72, 73, 79, 91
Spraggon, Monsignor, 87
Squires, P T, 81
Steadman, Ralph, 95
Steen, Vernon, 45
Stewart, Nora Kinzer, 95
Stirling, David, 55
Stockton-on-Tees, *87*
Strange, Ian, 87
Supporting Arms Co-ordination Centre, 49
Sussex Mountain, 25
Swan Inlet, 64

Teal Inlet, 23, 25, 27, 28, 45, *45*, 48, 49, 51, 63, 66, *68*, 70, 78, 80
Thatcher, Margaret, 5, 61, 86, 89, 93
Thomas, John, 63
Thompson, Julian, 19-39, 41, 55, 89
Thorne, Sir David, 81-88, *82*, *84*
Top Malo House, 28
Two Sisters, 17, 29-33, *33*, 36, 47, 51, 70

Underwood, Geoffrey, 90
United States, 12, 95

Vaux, Nick, 34

Wall Mountain, 34
Washington, Brian, *99*
Welch, Anthony, 76-80
Weston, Simon, 93
Wheeler, Roger, 82
Whitehead, Andrew, 25, 32-3
Wideawake Airfield, 62
Winfield, Ian, 89
Wilson, Anthony, 27-8, 35
Wireless Ridge, 17, 29-32, 35, 37-9, *38*, 43, 46, 47, 51, 60
Witherow, John, 90
Woodward, Sir John 'Sandy', 7-8, 13-15, 29
Wratten, W J, 81
Wreford-Brown, Christopher, 90